Total Life Prosperity

TOTAL LIFE

LANSON

TYNDALE HOUSE PUBLISHERS, INC.

Prosperity

ROSS

WHEATON, ILLINOIS

Second printing, March 1983
Library of Congress Catalog Card Number 82-50798
ISBN 0-8423-7293-8

This book is dedicated to

RALPH BRUKSOS

a man who was spiritual enough

to tell me the truth about myself.

CONTENTS

P A R T   F O U R
HOW TO MAKE DECISIONS IN A CRISIS HOUR

P A R T   F I V E
YOUR PROSPERITY PERSONALITY

INTRODUCTION

For three years I had been director of public affairs and then vice-president of King's Garden in Seattle, Washington, now known as Crista Ministries. At thirty-nine years of age, when things seemed to be going well, I resigned.

I wish I could say that I had left and moved on to bigger and better things. The painful truth is I had created a situation for the president of King's Garden, Dr. Clarence Reimer, that made it impossible for me to stay.

Some of my work of handling the mission's public relations, development, and the mission department had been very successful. In fact, I found out later that it was my inability to handle success that had driven me to create such a pressure situation that Dr. Reimer would rather have me gone than working with him. I had yet to learn how success could bring failure.

King's Garden was no different from other positions with churches and ministries I had held. As the work I did became more and more successful, I would lose my temper more and more often because of my personal insecurities. At such times I would refuse counsel from others and try to force my will on those around me. Depression would then set in, and the morbid side of my personality would begin to dominate.

Usually my downfall would be in board meetings, pastoral meetings, or church conventions. I would make it known that I thought they were dumb, boring, and if they would let me run them I could do a better job. Finally I would begin to insult my peers until they turned from me. I would have a temper tantrum and either literally stomp out of a meeting in a huff or I would leave mentally by putting my mind into neutral.

In spite of what happened, even to this day I love and respect Clarence Reimer as one of the greatest men I have ever known. Never would I have wanted to hurt him, and yet I am sure that I did. But it had become my pattern to hurt those I loved the most, including my wife and family.

Frequent changes of jobs and affiliations had been a part of my life. Part of my ministry was with the Presbyterian Church. I had studied at a Conservative Baptist seminary, taking their pretheology course. I had graduated from a Free Methodist college, been ordained in a General Association of Regular Baptist church, preached as an interdenominational evangelist, and finally transferred my ordination to the Evangelical Free Church. All this moving had not allowed me to put down firm roots anywhere. In fact, when I left King's Garden, I had neither a job nor a retirement plan. And, at the time, I felt I did not have much of a future either. All that was certain was that we would continue to live in Seattle. I was determined that my sons would have a solid base from which to develop.

I had begun my ministry at the age of eighteen when I was licensed to preach at the Mayger (Oregon) Community Church. At thirty-nine, I was still committed to God, but not committed to any kind of ministry.

For the first time in my adult life I was free from boards, committees, bosses, and congregations. The problem was that I had no training to do anything but minister. Upon this sea of newfound freedom, I launched several projects, hoping one or more would prove financially seaworthy in order to build some kind of a future for me and my family.

Within a few weeks I had started a fund-raising company, a corporation with a partner building new homes, a corporation with a partner fixing up old homes, a partnership developing a piece of raw land, and finally another partnership buying and selling older homes.

To make a long story short, in six months I could hardly find the top of my desk. There was no time for myself, my family, friends, or even God. At times in my life I had been in messes but never anything like this one. Phone calls were not being answered. Letters went weeks and even months without reply. In fact, at one point when I traveled, I carried two and sometimes three briefcases full of correspondence, proposals, reports, calls, and detail work that I could not or would not get finished.

Something had to be done. In desperation I hired a consultant to help me learn how to manage my affairs. For about twenty months we would meet every Friday to talk about how I could solve my business problems.

We talked about everything. The consultant put a great deal of emphasis on people with whom I chose to work. He kept pressing me about the people I had hired or with whom I had gone into business. It was his contention that some of them were losers and that I must have some weakness in my personality that caused me to surround myself with losers.

I became irritated when he talked to me about my mother, father, and my home life. He kept asking about the churches I had pastored, the positions I had held, and why I thought I had left each one. I remember telling him, "I did not hire you as a shrink. Tell me how to straighten out these businesses, PERIOD. Teach me about financial reports, trends of the money market, and how to spot a business opportunity."

Still, time and time again, for over ten months, he came back to what had taken place in each ministry position I had served until finally one day he dropped the bomb. Literally this book and my life as it is today have risen out of the ashes left when the bomb exploded. He told me what was wrong in my life.

"Lanson, you are a genius," he started out, "but you have programmed yourself for failure and you never will be worth much as a person or to God until you understand that and do something about it."

He went on to point out that in each instance of my ministry I had worked with problems and difficulties. He told me I was a problem solver, but every time I moved a program to where it was a success I would push the panic button, create a situation so that the people with whom I worked did not want to continue the association, or I would just leave.

I really got angry when he said, "The things wrong in your life and your businesses are not anybody else's fault but your own." At this I exploded. Jumping to my feet, I said, "You are no shrink so get off my back. Get out of my head and teach me how to run these businesses."

His reply will never be forgotten. "Lanson, sit down and shut up. For once in your life, listen to someone else. You have such a massive ego that nobody can tell you anything. Now sit down, shut up, and I'll do what you hired me to do."

For the next hour and more, in love, he outlined for me the problem of my life in bringing a program to a place of success, but even when I was succeeding I still saw myself as a failure. So he said, "You have to push the pressure button and get things so confused people would rather have you gone, even though they might need your gifts and abilities. Because you see yourself as a failure, you can't live with success." What came through to me was that he felt I had great ability but I made others pay such a price they were happy to see me gone from their team.

When the session was over I left, slamming the door as I went. I had seldom been so angry. All the way down the elevator I was fuming. As I left the lobby, my temper got the best of me and I turned around to go back up to his twelfth-floor office to "punch his lights out." Fortunately the elevator was gone. Before it arrived back at the lobby, I said to myself, "Lanson, this is what he was talking about, pushing the pressure button and leaving."

Out the door I went and started the six blocks to my car. The more I walked the more angry I became. "He can't talk to me that way," I thought. "I don't care what he said, I'm going back down there and deck him." After retracing my steps for about two blocks I stopped and again said, "This is the type of behavior Ralph was talking about when he told you your ego was out of control."

Turning again, I walked to my car and headed home. Perhaps you can identify with the scene that followed. I walked in the door of my home, obviously upset. My wife naturally asked what was wrong. In anger I replied, "Nothing is wrong," adding sarcastically, "Why do you think something is wrong?" Wisely she remained quiet.

The next six days were hell around our house. I entered my usual "take it out on the wife, kids, and dog" behavior. Finally, on Thursday night, I repented and took Mary out for a nice Chinese dinner. As we sat eating, Mary asked quietly what had been bothering me all week. Now I felt was my chance. I would tell her all these terrible things the consultant had said about me. She would agree with me that he was a jerk and I should never go back to see him. Then would come all the positive strokes I needed for my wounded male ego.

I told her all the things he had said and how angry I had been and how I turned back twice to return and punch him. After a pause she said quietly, "But, honey, you know he's right."

The truth had been spoken. I was judged by it and now found myself in deep need—emotionally, mentally, and spiritually.

Out of that painful awakening a new life has taken shape.

This book tells how it happened. If I felt I was the only person who had gone through these problems, such a book would be unnecessary. But I suspect that many others have come to just a place in their lives and are looking, as I was, for some answers.

PART ONE
SELF-IMAGE
IS BASIC
TO YOUR
DEVELOPMENT

1 / Looking Inside

"Take a look at this," my wife said with a laugh. She was trying to get me to stop whatever I was doing, or running to do, to show me a school paper my youngest son had brought home from the first grade.

His teacher had asked the students to write a paper about themselves. Actually the paper was to tell of some experience they had had during spring vacation. It was the title my son Lanny gave his paper that had caused Mary to chuckle. As I read it I made a feeble effort to laugh. In truth the title had cut me to my deepest level of emotion.

The title of his paper was "Marvelous Me."

I was so moved I went up to my bedroom and sat on the bed and tried to read his little paper. I couldn't get past the title, the tears were coming so hard. I began to pray. "Oh, God, how could my son feel so good about himself and I feel so bad about my life?" At age six my son had a better image of himself than I had at age thirty-three. It was my poor self-image that was causing me pain.

At the time I was considered the successful pastor of the First Evangelical Free Church in Vancouver, Washington, and yet I felt lousy. The church was growing and people were being converted. We had won the denomination's Sunday

School of the Year award. I had every reason to feel happy, but I wasn't. I was so mixed up emotionally that I was not aware my misery came as a result of a poor self-image.

FORGIVENESS DOESN'T CHANGE SELF-IMAGE

That it is possible to be forgiven and still feel bad about myself I didn't yet understand. Ahead of me were the experiences that would open my mind to understand how one can have a measure of success in his vocation and calling but still have a low opinion of himself.

BEING CALLED DOESN'T CHANGE SELF-IMAGE

By the time I was thirty-three I had experienced some exciting moments in the ministry. The night I was licensed to preach at age eighteen, people had walked the aisle to be saved. The congregation was told that this was a sign of God's approval of my being licensed at such an early age. I suppose it could have been true. I do know the church I was licensed to serve experienced growth from the beginning. During this time I was studying in Portland, Oregon.

In the early days of my ministry, I felt I was over my head, but I hoped that when I got older my feelings of inadequacy would leave me, that somehow I would grow out of these insecure feelings. Some of the most exciting days of my life were the three years I spent as the youth director at Hillcrest Presbyterian Church while attending Seattle Pacific College. The privilege to preach each Sunday night as well as work with the youth gave me experience afforded few twenty-one-year-old ministerial students.

During these days, I married Mary Freleigh, in December of 1957. My wife has such a good self-image! One might think it would have helped me, but it didn't. As an excellent marimbist, Mary had received many positive strokes. This didn't help me any, since I became Mary's husband, the packer and unpacker of the marimba. We became a team, Mary playing and me packing and preaching.

To understand how deeply ingrained my poor self-image was, one would have to know the depth and strength of my call from God. After college came ordination, then twenty months of work as an evangelist. In sixteen states we saw people come to Christ, in big city churches and small country churches, city-wide meetings and small rural missions. It was a joy to see all kinds of people, alcoholics to athletes, find forgiveness.

In spite of all this success, I was miserable. There were times of fun, thrill, and blessing. But no matter what God did through me I was sure no one really liked me. At home my wife lived with a jealous fool, an explosive temper, a man very unsure of himself and insecure. I'm certain that Mary has jewels reserved in heaven for her crown for what she endured in those days.

Our oldest son David was born during our days in evangelism. Still we stayed on the road, towing our home behind us. Many are the times that Mary and I have talked about the meeting in Baker, Montana, when it was 38° below zero and everything in our trailer home froze solid.

As David grew older, traveling became more difficult, so we settled down for a while when I became pastor of the Church of the Open Door in Nampa, Idaho.

Here in Nampa our second son, Lanson III (Lanny), was born. The church grew but my problems remained the same, of course, always hidden from the people. All this time I was certain no one really liked me—not even my family.

Jesus said, "Love your neighbor as much as you love yourself" (Matthew 22:39). It is hard to describe how difficult it was to keep reaching out to people when I, myself, was so unhappy. The frustration of feeling unloved because I wouldn't love myself caused me to do and say many things I later regretted.

Excitement has always been a part of my life, so I wasn't sitting around pouting. Adventure for me is a way of life.

Adventure can come almost anytime if we are willing to pay the price. By the time I was twenty-seven, I had pastored in Idaho for two years, had earned my private pilot's license, nearly lost my life rafting through the Bruneau Canyon, and made a parachute jump just to see if I had the nerve to jump out of the plane when the time came.

There is a great difference between activity and self-acceptance. Somehow I must have reasoned in my mind that if I could do enough unusual things, enough good things, enough outstanding things, then people would recognize me, accept me, and even love me. In my mind, I needed continually to prove myself.

In each place of ministry we witnessed the moving of God's Spirit in people's lives. Yet my temper continued to wreak havoc. My wife suffered constantly trying to deal with my moody disposition. Mary felt she was walking on egg shells. When nearby Mt. St. Helens exploded, Mary was not too concerned. She had already lived through more than twenty years of the eruptions of my temper.

People who watched me and admired me had a hard time recognizing that all these conflicts were going on inside me. I had heard the comment many times: "You reach out to everyone. You are a very loving person." Little did they realize how empty I was and how I wanted to be able to allow someone to reach out to me. Yet how could I, since my ego, my self-image, was so fragile.

Over and over I had said to my wife, "Let's just quit. I'm tired of this. I can't really help anyone. Let's just forget it."

SUCCESS IN THE EYES OF OTHERS
WON'T CHANGE OUR SELF-IMAGE
In 1964, the door opened for an unusual challenge. Through my friend Dr. Clifford Clark of the Tulsa Baptist Temple, I was introduced to the work of the annual missionary con-

ference and the work of the Wycliffe Bible Translators.

After speaking at Dr. Clark's missions conference, I went back to Idaho to put on my first missions conference at the Church of the Open Door. At the conclusion of the conference we had a commitment well over our goal of $2,500. Previously we had been giving five dollars a month to a national working in India.

Arlo Heinrich of Wycliffe Bible translators told me of the need for a plane in Brazil and that our extra $2,400 could go toward it. As a pilot, I became interested in the need for this plane. In prayer I sensed God gave me a plan to raise the $25,000 needed for this aircraft.

In October of 1964, I invited Oswald J. Smith from the People's Church in Toronto to come to Idaho to speak at five dinners. By combining the faith-promise offering with a dinner program, over $27,000 was pledged in one week.

If ever I was going to feel good about myself it should have been at that point. At twenty-nine years of age, I had put together a successful project for one of the Lord's finest mission agencies. It was a thrill to be traveling and working with Dr. Smith, a great missionary statesman.

But again I felt threatened. My abilities were bringing another success and my personal insecurity was covered by my ego which projected myself as an authority in fund raising. Again this led to my next problem. Though others viewed me as a success, I continued to see myself as a failure and I had to get away from the people who knew me before they discovered that I really was a no-good person. I felt I had no right to feel good about myself. After all, pride is a sin. Little did I realize that pride and acceptance of oneself and the building of a good self-image are very different issues.

The faith-promise dinner ideas had been so successful that the chairman of the Jungle Aviation and Radio Service (JAARS) board challenged me to leave my church and lead an organization he was calling OPERATION 2000. He wanted me to raise money for projects for the Wycliffe Bible Translators and their air arm, JAARS.

This change called for a move to Greensboro, North Carolina, which gave me a good excuse to escape another success before I "failed." For the next eighteen months I traveled the United States from corner to corner, Bellingham to Miami and Philadelphia to San Diego, putting on dinners. Dr. Smith joined me for each of the thirty-seven dinners. From that small beginning in Idaho, the dinner concept has spread to bless many, many Christian organizations. OPERATION 2000 was God's instrument to break the ground for the Wycliffe Associates. This one organization has raised millions of dollars to bless thousands of people, using the dinner idea.

SUCCESS? YES. HAPPINESS? NO.

When we closed OPERATION 2000 some wondered why I did not consider moving into the program known as Wycliffe Associates. At a board meeting in North Carolina some criticism was leveled at portions of the program I had been doing. As I look back, the statements were legitimate and actually good suggestions. I became so upset that someone would dare to attack me and what I had done I blew up. Actually they were not attacking me, but my poor self-image made me feel that way. I made a fool out of myself at the meeting. I told them if they did not like the way I ran the program that I was quitting. Little did I realize that there were people who would take the program, improve it, and build it broader than I ever could.

I raised my voice, shook my fist, and finally turned on my heel, stomped out of the meeting, got into my car, and left.

PROGRAMMED FOR FAILURE

I truly was programmed for failure. I saw myself as a failure and unconsciously I seized opportunities to tell people off, stomp out, and not deal with the hard issues and questions. God used my abilities and caused success to come. Still I viewed myself as a failure, not believing I could maintain that level of accomplishment. I would push the pressure button and cause some frustration that made those in authority feel that they were better off without me. And they were.

Quitting OPERATION 2000 in a fit of rage, I was too weak in my own personality to apologize. I made my life miserable again by moving to the First Evangelical Free Church in Vancouver, Washington. It was a church of thirty-two members, with no place to go but up.

It was there, at thirty-three years of age, that I sat on my bed crying, with my son's paper in my hand, pouring out my heart to God about how miserable I felt about myself. How I wished I were able to write about some experiences I had been through which I could entitle "Marvelous Me," as my first-grader had done! Mine would have read "Miserable Me." Why was I like this? Where had this self-image problem started?

YOU WILL NEVER AMOUNT TO ANYTHING

Anne Ortlund has written a book titled: *Children Are Like Wet Cement* (Old Tappan, NJ: Revell, 1981). One does not need to be a trained psychologist to understand that if someone tells a young person something over and over again while the cement of his life is still wet, so to speak, he is going to believe it, even if what the child is told is wrong.

My mother was a strong, innovative person of unusual strengths and weaknesses. Her ten children, seven boys and three girls, made sure she learned a lot about rearing children.

How stunned my wife was when we went to visit my mother. We had forgotten David's baby high chair. My mother simply set a box upside down in an old straight-backed kitchen chair. Quick as a wink, David was on the box with a large dish towel tied around him and the slats in the chair back. With a big smile on his face, he was sitting up at the table with the rest of us.

What a baby-sitter! Whatever grandma was doing, the boys were doing. If she washed dishes, they washed dishes. "Come on now, help me cook dinner," she would say. What a mess they would make stirring mixing bowls of food. When she painted the house, they painted.

My mother is gone now. I preached her funeral, but that is another story. It was one of those times when I was overpowered and undergirded simultaneously by the filling of the Holy Spirit of God. Sometimes in the middle of the night I miss my mother.

Most of what she would do wrong in the process of "growing up her kids," as she used to call it, was done in simple ignorance. She built many things into my life that were good for me, but some that were very bad. Among them was the poor self-image that plagued me for years. I want to believe that if mother had understood, she would never have done it.

I BECAME WHAT I HEARD I WAS

My mother used to say, "You are just like your dad." Or, "I guess I shouldn't expect much from you. After all, you are named for your dad." There were other expressions I don't want to repeat.

From where I stand now, on this side of childhood and adolescence, I know my mother was trying to correct me. Some of what she said was done in anger, some in deep frustration, and some as a warped kind of discipline.

For whatever the reason, the effect was the same. In my mind I was expected to perform no better than my father, and his personal record wasn't too good.

Lanson C. Ross, Sr., my father, was a brilliant man. I realized this when he lived with Mary and me the last nine years of his life. But as a child I knew him as a heavy drinker who at times made our lives miserable at home. He would come home drunk and he and mother would fight, both verbally and sometimes physically. On occasion Dad would pack up and move out. He would stay in the same town and keep working but he would stay away from home for weeks and sometimes months.

MY MIND WAS PROGRAMMED FOR FAILURE

My memory is clear. I have slept with a knife under my pillow, hoping my father would come home and start a fight so I could cut him and make him feel as bad as I felt. At times I really hated him, yet I was being told I was just like him. It is no wonder I hated myself.

At the time I could feel only anger at a violent father. It took years for me to turn hate into understanding of my father, a man who himself had been a victim of a poor self-image.

Knowing these things about me, people aren't surprised to learn that as a senior in high school I was found drunk in class one day and expelled from school.

That could have been the end of me, except for one of my teachers. Mrs. Esther Kelly, a godly woman, didn't give up on me. At that time I didn't understand her but I did respect her very highly. The day after I was expelled from school, Mrs. Kelly took me to the civic auditorium in Portland, Oregon, to hear a man preach. There is no way to describe what happened to me as I sat in the front row of the third balcony. Along with 5,500 other people I listened to a prophet of encouragement pour out his heart, telling me how to know the Lord.

The Holy Spirit walked those aisles and touched my heart, mind, and emotions. As Dr. Merv Rosell gave the invitation, I walked to the prayer and counsel room and gave my life and my eternity into the keeping of Jesus Christ.

My father-in-law has summed up well my feelings about conversion. He said, "The hardest thing in the Bible to understand is not Ezekiel and his wheels, not Gog and Magog, nor Daniel and his seventy weeks, but John 3:16:

'For God loved the world so much that he gave his only Son so that anyone who believes in him shall not perish but have eternal life.'" I'll never understand why God loved me so much that his Son Jesus died for me. But I am thankful he did.

YOU CAN EXPERIENCE SALVATION AND STILL SUFFER

Forgiveness is fabulous, but it did not change how I viewed myself. Of course, an all-powerful God could forgive me, but I felt I had no right to expect anyone else to forgive me and accept me. After all, I needed to be forgiven. I was no good, just like my father. Mother had said so for seventeen years, and I believed her.

Looking back, I can almost divide my life story by decades. The first ten years of my Christian life, I believed at face value what I was told about the Christian life and how to live it. Most of what I was told was about the things that I shouldn't do—the negative side. So I lived negatively. It was easy for me, since I already had a poor self-image. I was effective in my ministry during those years, but I was miserable. Worse yet, I could not admit it to anybody, not even myself. When one is preaching peace and joy, one can't let people know that he himself is miserable. After ten years of living and serving as a Christian, I have to say I didn't really enjoy the Christian life, period.

It may not make sense to some when I say that I loved the Lord God with all my heart, mind, soul, and strength, but I did not enjoy being a negative person. Now I know that the negative mind-set I had was causing me to do less than my best with the gifts God had given to me to use. During those years, I felt terribly unfulfilled.

The next ten years, from age twenty-nine to thirty-nine, I set out on an adventure of faith. It took me this second ten-year period to learn what the Christian life is and how it operates. My faith came into focus when I realized that Christianity is not a church nor a creed, not a denomination

nor a doctrine, not a regulation nor a rule book, but a relationship—a relationship between me and Almighty God,
provided for me by the death and resurrection of his Son
Jesus Christ, a relationship nurtured as I yielded myself to
the Holy Spirit.

AN IMPROVED SELF-IMAGE
WILL ALTER YOUR LIFE

During these years of the third decade, I have been learning
that one cannot build a good relationship with anyone else
unless one feels good about himself. Unless a person has a
good self-image the relationship with one's wife or husband
will suffer. Children will become a part of the suffering. Jobs
that one loves and wants to keep may be snatched away.
Yes, even relationships to God will be out of focus and service for Christ will suffer.

There was a way out of this swamp of self-pity and despair
and you can discover it too. God wants our self-image to improve. Paul wrote: "And I am sure that God who began the
good work within you will keep right on helping you grow in
his grace until his task within you is finally finished on that
day when Jesus Christ returns" (Philippians 1:6).

God does not want us to have a poor self-image. He has
made it clear that a man is to think good of himself. The
Psalmist wrote: "Lord, you are my shield, my glory, and
my only hope. You alone can lift my head, now bowed in
shame" (Psalm 3:3). God has made it possible for us to
change the way we view ourselves.

Self-image can be altered. I know that mine has been.
Perhaps the greatest evidence to me that this has happened is
being able to share openly with you in this book what God
has led me to do about raising the level of my self-esteem.

2 / The View Looking Out

Many times I have wished I were someone else. Always life has seemed easier for others than for me. But each time I allow myself to play in the sandbox of self-pity, I am brought back to reality, realizing that such a thing can never be possible.

THERE IS NOT GOING TO BE ANOTHER ME

Body. I have no body to work with but the one that now houses my soul. Part of my problem historically has been that I did not feel myself worthy of the effort to take care of my body. Proper diet, weight control, and exercise were not a part of my life. It just didn't seem worth it.

It is quite obvious from the Scriptures that the Lord had saved me for a reason. I remained alive for a purpose. Paul settled that for me when he wrote: "Sometimes I want to live and at other times I don't, for I long to go and be with Christ. How much happier for me than being here! But the fact is that I can be of more help to you by staying! Yes, I am still needed down here and so I feel certain I will be staying on earth a little longer, to help you grow and become happy in your faith" (Philippians 1:23-25).

Emotions. While I remain here on earth I have no other emotions to build on except mine. When they get out of control I can't trade them in for a new set. When they run down in depression, and they do, it is my responsibility to tune them up and get moving again.

Energy. It would be nice if I could plug into someone else's energy, but all I have available is what I can develop with the body and mind God gave me. In America when we say all men are created equal, we mean our souls have equal worth in the sight of God and other lofty and noble concepts. It doesn't mean that my wife and I both like to get up in the morning. She likes to stay up; I like to get up.

Mind. For years I was convinced I was a dolt, about one step above stupid. Mary was a member of the National Honor Society for scholastic excellence. Not only was I not a member, but I had to stop and look up the word *scholastic* to make sure I spelled it correctly. I remember people saying that Einstein said he used only 15 percent of his brain capacity. How could he be so smart on 15 percent when I was sure I was using 90 percent and still felt inferior? Yet what was I to do? I had no mind except the one with which I was born.

Perhaps you can identify with me in wishing for more mind capacity, fuller energy, and altered personality, or a stronger emotional makeup. But you, like me, have experienced the feeling of being trapped because the only raw material available to you for building a life came as part of the package with which you arrived at birth. What I had in my package, very frankly, did not impress me, and I was in trouble.

Some fundamental questions about life face each of us— questions we must process and seek for answers:

First, there is the problem of *being,* a problem outlined in the question, Who am I? Along with these three words are all kinds of other questions, such as, Why am I here? What do I have to offer the world? Exactly what am I really like?

All of us have asked ourselves these questions and others as well.

The formative years are spent building the foundation from which to answer these questions. If the input the brain is receiving says, ''You are no good. You never will amount to anything.'' Or, ''You are just like . . .'' (somebody no good), then you perceive yourself as being no good.

Receiving and internalizing these messages are what can be called being ''programmed for failure.'' If someone sees himself as a failure then ability alone is not enough to turn such a person into a winner. Believing he is a failure will sooner or later put him on a road that will lead to a self-fulfilling prophecy and he will fail. Then he can say, ''I knew I couldn't do it.'' Thus he continually reinforces that poor self-image, that failure image he has of himself.

Acting out these false beliefs was my pattern for years. I use the past tense here, because I am no longer in that groove. Because of God's deliverance, I have left that rut, and I hope forever.

Second, there is the problem of *guilt*. When someone sees himself as a failure, he will try repeatedly to change, but unless he has a plan for changing, he will probably continue to fail. When he fails he will then feel guilty for letting himself down, failing others, and failing God.

We have all had some habit we would like to break. We call them bad habits. For some it may be smoking, nail biting, filthy language, or a multitude of other things. When we try to break out of habit's prison and fail, two things generally happen: we feel guilty, and we seem to get worse.

Combine the problem with the biblical truth of the basic sin nature of man and we have a tremendous battle on our hands. Is it any wonder I was expelled from high school as a senior for being drunk in class? Because of a personal disappointment of being dumped by my girl friend, my weak self-image was again reinforced. I went out to do what I had learned people do who think of themselves as failures—I got drunk. In my mind I was a failure and so again and again I had created situations that allowed me to fail. But this reaction did not take away the guilt.

Third, there is the problem of *rationalization*. By this I mean the excuses we make to justify what we have done in order to go on living with ourselves. When we do something wrong and guilt sets in, we must do something to alleviate the guilt or stop the criticism we fear may come as a result of what we have done. Rationalization becomes the tool we use to make our actions acceptable.

We make our actions tolerable by saying, "Well, what difference does it make as long as it doesn't hurt anybody else?" The phrase is heard often, "Everybody does it these days." We know we are in bad shape when we say, "I don't care." Deep down we do care, I'm convinced. For years when all else failed to bring me peace I would say, "I don't care." But real changes in self-image began when I admitted that I did care. When that happened I began to discover the positive things I could do to change—not just be challenged, but to change. If I can change, if my self-image can be altered, if my self-esteem can rise, there is hope for others.

THEN I WAS BORN AGAIN

I would like to be able to tell people that when I was born again all my problems were solved. They weren't. I've heard the preaching that seems to say, "Be born again and the grass becomes greener, you float on a cloud, the trees are taller, and perfume smells sweeter." Not so.

Paul said, "When someone becomes a Christian he becomes a brand new person inside. He is not the same any more. A new life has begun!" (2 Corinthians 5:17). That verse is true; it happened to me. I received that new life. But Paul did not say that in this new life I would never have a problem. The verse does not say that everything we have thought and done is suddenly wiped from the memory.

The verse tells us that God forgives us and gives us the opportunity for knowing the one true foundation for living,

Jesus Christ. We now have the opportunity to build a new life. Rather than saying that we will never have another problem, it shows rather that we now have a foundation on which to build a life that will make us able to handle the problems that come. The key in Paul's statement is, "A new life has begun." This new life needs to be nurtured, educated, and directed. In short, we need to learn how to live this new life.

WHAT THE NEW LIFE IS

Someone might put up a mental block when he starts to read this section. We must not, however, stray from the truth of the Word of God. Buried within me now are deep feelings of frustration because of the way I learned to view the new life for the first ten years of my Christian life. There are several important truths about the new life that need to be considered in terms of our self-esteem.

First, we are sinners. "For all have sinned and come short of the glory of God" (Romans 3:23, KJV). This verse was the first passage read to me the night I was born again. It was true then and it is still true today. Those words have echoed through our churches and evangelistic meetings hundreds of thousands of times.

It took me twenty years of Christian living, nineteen of them preaching, to realize that the church was saying the same things to me my mother had said, only in different words. "Lanson, you are a sinner. Lanson, you are no good. You are just like your father."

We must understand what the Bible is saying to us. We must see the picture as it unfolds. The teaching I was receiving and giving was not solving my self-image problem. It was reinforcing it. The idea that "I am a no-good person" was what I lived with every day. The conflict—how do I describe the conflict! There were abilities God had given to me that, when used, brought about what others called successes. But the conflict remained. How could I ever be a success when I was such a bad person? To do successful things and to be a success are two different things.

Second, the battle with guilt remained. In fact, in some ways it was worse. Before I found the new life in Christ I failed myself. Now I was also failing the Almighty God.

There was no problem in understanding what Paul wrote to the Romans: "It seems to be a fact of life that when I want to do what is right, I inevitably do what is wrong. I love to do God's will so far as my new nature is concerned, but there is something else deep within me, in my lower nature, that is at war with my mind and wins the fight and makes me a slave to the sin that is still within me. In my mind I want to be God's willing servant but instead I find myself still enslaved to sin.

"So you see how it is: my new life tells me to do right, but the old nature that is still inside me loves to sin. Oh, what a terrible predicament I'm in! Who will free me from my slavery to this deadly lower nature? Thank God! It has been done by Jesus Christ our Lord. He has set me free" (Romans 7:21-25).

I think many Christians view the Christian life the way I did. We believe the Bible but our lives tell us we are in a battle with sin and much of the time we lose. Then we feel guilty before God and man.

In my early Christian experience, so much of the teaching I received was negative and legalistic. I had more things to be guilty about after I was born again than before.

It is possible to be born again and still not have a good self-image because we may continue to battle guilt feelings. For me it was a continuation of the same problems of who I was (you are a sinner, Lanson) and look what I've done now (guilty before God and man).

Third, as believers we go from rationalizing to spiritualizing. We agree with Paul: "Oh, what a terrible predicament I'm in! Who will free me from my slavery to this deadly lower nature? Thank God! It has been done by Jesus Christ our Lord. He has set me free." But herein lies a problem. If

Jesus has solved this dilemma for me, why do I still do things that are wrong? Once again we must justify our actions. So, we spiritualize.

As a pastor I have heard some dandy statements by people trying to spiritualize the things they do. In fact, I've used some myself. Perhaps you will recognize some of the statements as well: "I know I shouldn't do this, but I have prayed about it, and God doesn't take it away." Or, "It must be wrong. The Bible says so, but even prayer doesn't seem to help." I have heard these used to excuse immorality. Another one is, "If God wants me to amount to something then he will make me into it. In the meantime I just go on living."

The problem with spiritualizing is the same as with rationalizing. We are attempting to excuse our actions. Someone has said that excuses have a time limit. The older they are the weaker they become.

To begin a healing process in our lives and to change how we view ourselves, we need to accept the fact that the gospel does not make us less accountable simply because God has entered the picture. It makes us more accountable. The writer of Hebrews said: "Since we have such a huge crowd of men of faith watching us from the grandstands, let us strip off anything that slows us down or holds us back, and especially those sins that wrap themselves so tightly around our feet and trip us up; and let us run with patience the particular race that God has set before us" (Hebrews 12:1).

One of the great sins today is the attitude, "What are you going to do about my problem?" People are asking, "What is the school going to do about my problem? What is the church going to do about my problem? What is the government going to do about my problem? What is God going to do about my problem?"

The real question is, "What are you going to do about your problem?"

I have sinned before God and man, and basic to my problem was a self-image that convinced me I was a loser. Jesus has set us free. We have been freed in two ways. There is the freedom from guilt and punishment of sin eternally. Also, we have a foundation in Christ which we can build on with a motivation given us by the Holy Spirit to accept the responsibility for our actions. Maturity is accepting the responsibility for the things we have done and said.

There is no question that man is a sinner. All of us have striven to please God and have felt guilty when we failed. Some of us tried to spiritualize—to explain our behavior so we could still live with ourselves in spite of what we did.

But understanding a few basic principles and applying them to our lives can solve the problem of how to change one's self-image.

3 / The View Looking Up

Many times I have been asked, "How can I change? Where do I start?" My answer is always the same. "Begin at the beginning." For me this was rediscovering the Creator, the One who had made me the way I am.

It seems very trite to say, "Your self-image can change." But after more than twenty years living as a Christian, I suddenly discovered five years ago that I really could change, and that it was all right with God for me to change. In fact, He wanted me to be different and had made provision so that my self-image could change.

In my search for the principles of living up to my potential, I read and reread Genesis 1:26: "Then God said, 'Let us make a man—someone like ourselves, to be the master of all life upon the earth and in the skies and in the seas.'"

Words fail me in describing what took place in my life when it dawned on me that God made us like him. I realize we are still sinners with the ability to sin, but if we are created in the image of God, if we are like him, it means we have basic worth. We are worth something! Though we were lost, the born-again experience opens up to us access to the One who made us with basic worth, since we were made by him who is of infinite worth. May God help us, in our preaching and teaching, to take people beyond being sinners.

Let the healing come! "Lanson, you are like your father," I told myself—"your heavenly Father, not your earthly father."

MY MOTHER WAS WRONG

Just because I had heard something about myself for years, that didn't make it true. God is not a liar. We are made in his image. We are God's unique creation. I don't believe he created us to go around feeling negative about ourselves day after day. God is not negative, for he constantly calls man to be realistic about life and to live in hope.

I DO HAVE ABILITIES

God, who made us, gave each of us abilities and gifts. When we see the Lord in the light of Genesis 1:26, it becomes plain that if I am to master the skies, the land, and the sea, he has given me the ability to do so.

To be able to do things and know that we can do them is not a matter of pride but of acknowledgment of being fashioned by the Creator, who has given us a task in life and the tools to complete it. We do not all have the same abilities nor do we have them in the same measure, nor do we all have the same kinds of tasks. The worst tragedy about the prison of a poor self-image is that it demeans God by not accepting the fact that he has given us abilities. A bad self-image keeps us thinking so negatively about ourselves that we neither accept the tasks he has given us nor the tools for the task.

We must not be concerned or covetous of another's abilities. We must determine to pay the price in self-discipline to see that those skills and gifts that we have are fully developed and used to honor the Lord. We mustn't settle for less and we must also realize that God doesn't expect more.

Admit it, there are things we can do. Some things we do very well, perhaps not as well as others, but for us these abilities are clearly God-given and intended to be used.

GOD LOVES US

The Lord has shown his love for us by allowing his Son to die for us. But his love goes deeper than simply this initial encounter. Continually he loves and accepts us.

Much of my life I have felt unlovely and unloved. God is to be praised, for he has a love for us that accepts us where we are. But his love doesn't leave us there. He has called us to growth and maturity.

GOD GIVES US OPPORTUNITY

In order for us to be masters as God has stated, we are not only equipped with abilities but we are also given opportunities. God is in the business of giving us chances to grow.

We often don't recognize God-given opportunities because they often come disguised either as difficulty, or hard work, or both. Someone has well said, "One man's problem is another man's opportunity." Many have said, "I wish I could fly." The Wright brothers did. Men everywhere declared the ocean too wide. Lindberg made it smaller by flying over it alone.

The key to walking in God's will is not "What am I supposed to do?" but rather, "How do I conduct myself so God gets the glory when I do what I know I can do?"

For years I heard and taught the way to know the will of God is to line up three lighthouses, so to speak. There is the lighthouse of God's Word, the lighthouse of circumstances, and the lighthouse of the inner witness of the Holy Spirit. When all three lighthouses are in line, then you can move safely through the storms of life into the harbor of God's will. Being the sailor that I am, I thought that sounded good. The only problem is that one of those lighthouses always seems not quite to line up, or it flickers, and I can't seem to get a steady reading, or worse yet, when I am ready to make my decision I look one final time and the light has gone out. It is seldom for me that all the feelings and circumstances line up perfectly at decision time.

Personally I have retired the lighthouse illustration about finding God's will. I've gone to a steady satellite signal, which is God's Word. The Bible tells me I am made in God's image, that I have worth. It tells me I have been given abilities to master the air, land, and sea, and I have been given opportunities. The real question for personal and spiritual growth, personal and spiritual maturity, and success in living is whether or not I do what I can for my own selfish end or for the honor, praise, and glory of God.

All of us must answer that question—are we going to do what we can do for our own ego satisfaction or for the honor of the Lord of glory?

The church I pastored had acquired a printing press. It had fallen to my lot to run this offset Goliath. One day a fine family came to the church. The man was an offset printer—in fact, the best in the area. He came to me and said, "Pastor, I'm not a teacher or a youth worker, but I can print, so why don't you let me run the press when I come to church for the midweek service?" Here was a man doing what he knew he could do and choosing to do it for the Lord's glory rather than his own gain.

What would happen if a church had mechanics who would say, "I'm going to find two widows and take care of their cars"? There is a scriptural admonition to care for the orphans and widows. The mechanics could put it on their calendars once per month to drive the widow's cars, and check the oil, brakes, and battery. When something needed to be fixed he could ask her to buy the parts and he would do the repairs. This could be done quietly as a tangible expression of his love for Jesus Christ and as a service to him.

Such ministry to one another in the church could be dangerous. When someone tells a widow someone wants to keep her car in good repair she may die of a heart attack. But in many cases people in the church would start lining up, not just to be served but to serve others.

Good things happen for us when we do what we can as a service to the Lord. We begin to see ourselves differently as well as understand better the gifts God has given to us. The will of God for each of us is to join what we know we can do to the opportunity God gives us to use what comes of that union for his honor and glory.

CALLED TO FREEDOM
God has not called us to go around feeling guilty and under a cloud of self-imposed condemnation. Paul wrote: "So there is now no condemnation awaiting those who belong to Christ Jesus" (Romans 8:1). The Lord wants us to be free from guilt and from condemnation, free to accomplish and to succeed. Jesus said, "You are truly my disciples if you live as I tell you to, and you will know the truth, and the truth will set you free" (John 8:31, 32).

Included in that process of being set free is the provision to change how we view ourselves. For me one of my insidious sins is to look on myself as a failure. This sin of low self-esteem has limited what I could have done with the abilities God has given me.

HOW YOU VIEW YOURSELF
When my "Marvelous Me" son was four or five, he was taking piano lessons from a lady in Vancouver, Washington. In an effort to encourage him she complimented him as he finished a piece by saying, "Lanny, that was perfect," to which my son replied, "Oh, no. No one is perfect but God. [Long pause.] But I did come pretty close." This young man has always had a strong self-image and it has allowed him to do some wonderful things.

When Lanny was fifteen he and I organized a bike trip on which he and another fifteen-year-old boy traveled from our home in Seattle to Washington, D.C. Lanny believed in himself enough to camp along the way and travel 4,400 miles in sixty-seven days.

When he was twelve he came home from camp and told me God wanted him to go to the Air Force Academy and serve God and the nation. Frankly, I didn't know whether to pray or salute. On his own, my son pursued that goal. The cross-country bike ride was made so he could meet senators and congressmen to tell them he wanted to go to the Air Force Academy.

It was his confidence in himself and the Lord that gave his mother and me courage to allow him to go during the summer of his sixteenth year to England and Scotland and tour for thirty days. On that trip he took his thirteen-year-old cousin with him. It was tough, but good for them.

It is amazing what we can do when we have a good self-image, one that will allow us to exercise our abilities in response to opportunities given us by God. It is important for us to grasp the principles for changing our self-image and start applying them.

What a thrill it was several years later when Lanny got a telegram reading, "Dear Lanson: The Air Force Academy has just notified me that they will be offering you an appointment to the class beginning in June of this year. Congratulations and best wishes. Sincerely, Joel Pritchard, Member of Congress."

Self-image is not destructive pride and ego out of control. A good self-image is the issue, and it is a fact that we accomplish more when we believe we have worth and ability, and then join them to God's opportunities.

4 / Five Steps to Change How You View Yourself

Thomas Harris, writing in *Reader's Digest,* said there are three things that make people want to change. They must hurt sufficiently, they must experience despair or boredom, or they must suddenly discover that they can change.

IT IS POSSIBLE TO CHANGE SELF-IMAGE

It is time to turn from the boredom of life, repudiate the hurts that have come, and awaken to discover that we, too, can change how we feel about ourselves.

MIND FOOD

The first thing one must do is to put oneself on a program of absorbing the right mind food. What do we read? To what do we listen? What are we feeding our minds?

Someone might say, "I don't like to read." It is not a question of whether or not we like it. We must do it. What we feed our minds will determine how we view ourselves.

Where did we get the view we have of ourselves? We drew the conclusions in our minds from the input we have received from many sources down through the years. Frankly, it is not valid for us to say, "My performance dictates my self-image." Just the opposite is true. Our self-image will dictate our performance.

The computer functions in some ways like a human brain. The computer people use an expression, "GIGO," which means, "Garbage in, garbage out." One can only get out of a computer what has been put into it. If the program or information entered is incorrect, the information the computer generates will not be worth anything.

Our brains function much the same way. A brain only processes the information it receives and then feeds it back. Many of us have been fed wrong information in the past and our brains keep feeding back wrong information when we ask for recall. Isaiah knew that his mind must be filled with thoughts of God if he expected to be strengthened with the knowledge of God in times of trouble. "He will keep in perfect peace those who trust in him, whose thoughts turn often to the Lord!" (Isaiah 26:3). Paul said, "Don't copy the behavior and customs of this world, but be a new and different person with a fresh newness in all you do and think. Then you will learn from your own experience how his ways will really satisfy you" (Romans 12:2). Change the way we think? How? We· do so by reprogramming our minds, by giving our minds new input on which to build and draw conclusions.

I was startled when I read that each person in the United States spends each year an average of $311 on personal appearance. These dollars go to the beauty and barber shops, for the razors, creams, cleansers, sprays, and scents we use. Almost every penny of that $311 ($1,244 for a family of four) is spent from the neck up. Think of it! One might well ask how much a family of four spends from the ears in.

Paul, near the time of his execution, wrote with great meaning to his friend Timothy, "When you come, be sure to bring the coat I left at Troas with Brother Carpus, and also the books, but especially the parchments" (2 Timothy 4:13). The apostle indicated he valued his mind food as highly as the comfort of his physical body.

The technology of tape recording is a gift from God. When we think of mind food, we should also think of the value of tapes. Everyone ought to own and use a cassette player. Driving time ought to be used to feed our minds. Just before buckling up for safety, we should turn on the tape recorder to help produce a changed self-image by listening to mind-building taped messages. The average driving time to and from work is twenty-one minutes each way. That time could be well used to feed the mind rather than allow our minds to wander through the same negative input it has received from the past or the abuse of a hard day's work from which we keep drawing the same wrong and negative conclusions.

If we are really struggling with a poor self-image or a negative attitude, for the next sixty days we should try avoiding one piece of mind food, the newspaper. If we examine newspapers carefully we find section after section and story after story of nothing but problems and negative input. Yet how many people start their day with a cup of coffee and the newspaper! From the first good hours of the day, they start feeding their minds with negative things of life.

To change our self-image the first thing we need to do is to get on a program of feeding our minds good food every day.

SOUL FOOD

People see themselves in a better light and their self-image improves when they are right with God. We need a consistent source of growth food for our soul's benefit. Study courses involving us with the Word of God are available everywhere. We may receive a correspondence course from one of our favorite Bible schools or Christian institutions, or from the local Bible bookstore. We may want to be a part of a Bible study group taught at many local churches. The important thing is that we must get busy feeding our spiritual lives so they will grow.

I recall being at Cannon Beach Bible Conference in 1957 when a man spoke to the Bible teacher, a lovely lady from the South. He was concerned about his spiritual life and wanted to improve. I'll never forget standing and watching as he spoke to her. She reached out and very politely but sternly tapped on top of his overly large stomach and said, "How many times a day do you feed that?"

He said, "Well, I always have breakfast, and then at the job salesmen come in and once or twice in the morning we go out for coffee and doughnuts. I have lunch, maybe a couple of meetings with salesmen in the afternoon, dinner, and then I like to munch on something while I watch TV in the evening."

"Oh," the speaker said. "How often do you feed your soul? How many times a day do you read the Word of God and talk to God in prayer?"

The man answered, "Well, you see, that's what I'm trying to tell you—I have trouble with that."

To this she replied, "Well, I think your problem is that you have a fat belly and a skinny soul."

It is true. We try to take in spiritual concepts by listening only, not feeding on thoughts gained through reading and studying as means of input into our spiritual lives. If we have never been on a program to feed our spiritual lives, let me suggest a simple one. Buy the small pocket-size book of *Living Proverbs* and read one chapter per day. Most months have thirty-one days and Proverbs has thirty-one chapters, a chapter for each day. So, on the tenth of the month, for example, we might read chapter ten, and so on. In this way we can read our way through the book in the next thirty-one days. We will find Proverbs to be rich material for building a planned life-style. It will motivate us. It is good soul food.

Fulton J. Sheen said, "The mind is like a clock that is constantly running down and must be wound up daily with good thoughts." That's the need for mind food.

Soul food can be taken into our lives only if we take the time to follow through on a reading and study program. We don't have time? Teddy Roosevelt said, "Nine-tenths of wisdom consists of being wise in the scheduling of our time."

PHYSICAL FOOD

Wouldn't it be wonderful if the new birth achieved at salvation gave us a new metabolism rate!

I am not proud to say that at one point in my life I weighed 255 pounds. At this writing I am at 216. Frankly, I feel much better about myself at 216 than I did at 255. In the church we hear a lot about fellowship. I thought for years that fellowship meant coffee and doughnuts.

When I got serious about weight loss I went out and purchased a used doctor's scales, one of those with the balances on the top for determining weight to the quarter of a pound. For me it was one of the best things I have ever done for my physical condition. I would get discouraged getting on the kind of scales we buy from the local department store, the kind you step on three times and each time it registers a different weight. One has to step on it three times, add the total and divide by three and guess. It was too uncertain for me. I wanted to know daily what I weighed to the quarter of a pound. When the weight starts to go up, then I stand up sooner at the meal table.

"But I travel," someone may say. "I eat in restaurants three times a day. How do you expect me to lose weight?" We are good at justifying ourselves, rationalizing as to why we do what we do, as we read in the last chapter.

When I have to eat in restaurants on a business trip, I don't even look at the menu. I make up my mind before I go to the breakfast table I am going to have a grapefruit or a slice of melon and an English muffin, or whatever. I don't pick up the menu and wade through all the pancakes, strawberry waffles, and eggs benedict before I punish myself with a small order.

Maybe it is time you decided to have a hot fudge sundae on your birthday instead of all the days except your birthday. Sweets aren't my problem—it's the breads, the potato and gravy, pasta, and popcorn. I'll give you my pie any day for your garlic bread.

We must control our diet. We should decide now to

change our eating habits. We know exactly what we need to control if we are going to control our weight. We have no right to blame anyone else. The hand that holds the fork that is killing us is at the end of our arm!

We will feel better about ourselves. Our self-image will change when we get our weight where it should be.

BE A PARTICIPANT, NOT A SPECTATOR

Those who are striving for a good self-image are doers, not just viewers. We should concentrate on becoming a part of life, not simply watching it go by. It is unfortunate today that so much of our lives is spent viewing only.

When my sons were small it was interesting to observe them when they watched a lot of TV. Mary and I have been as guilty as some others. Due to our busy lives it became easy for us to use the TV as a baby-sitter. On Saturdays the boys would start with the cartoons and then just keep on watching. The only time there was participation on their part was at the commercial breaks and that was to argue and fight. From time to time, in disgust, I would turn off the TV and tell them to go outside and ride their bikes or go swimming, play catch, or go sailing. After about an hour of participating in some physical activity, one would come in and it seemed a new boy was showing up wearing my son's body.

We change how we view ourselves when we are participants. There should be something we like to do—swim, walk, jog, golf, sail, ski, basketball, camp, back pack, garden, climb, bowl. When we get back to doing, we will feel better about ourselves.

ACCEPT WHAT GOD IS DOING

We must understand that not everything about us can be changed, nor should it be. Paul had his thorn in the flesh that continually worked for his spiritual good.

The most frustrated people I know are those who are not

willing to accept things that cannot be changed. Many times as a pastor I have been asked the question, "Why? Why did God allow this? Why me, pastor? I've tried to do right."

To these questions I have only one answer: "Trust." Things that don't make sense here must make sense in eternity. My mother liked jigsaw puzzles. Sometimes she seemed to start in the middle and work all four ways. I used to wonder what she was doing, but finally it would make sense when I could see the completed picture.

We shouldn't bog down in life by battling things that will remain stagnant, or defy solution. There are some things my wife and I have agreed not to discuss. We will never change each other's minds, so we just accept one another's opinions. Life will make sense only when we one day see the completed eternal picture. We must learn not to agonize over and verbalize things we cannot change.

THOUGHT TO REMEMBER

As we work to change our self-image, we should remember that success is not how far we go but how far we have come from where we started.

I was born in a house in Killdeer, North Dakota, where they at one time tanned skunk hides. I'm a success not because of how far I have gone but I have come a long way from where I started.

Someday, when we get a chance to meet personally, as you shake my hand, take a good look at me. You will be seeing that kind of success, for God hasn't done anything for me that he can't do for you. Get to work on your self-image so that I can look on you as a success also.

A CHECKLIST TO LIFT YOUR IMAGE

Here is a list of things you can do right now to begin changing how you view yourself:

_____Clean your house, from top to bottom
_____Clean your office and keep it clean
_____Clean your car and keep it clean
_____Give away what you don't wear or use
_____Get up to date on all your correspondence
_____Get rid of anything that doesn't work
_____If you are owed something, or you owe
someone, come to an agreement or repayment
_____Return things you have borrowed
_____Balance your checkbook and keep it balanced
_____Get your family on a budget
_____Organize your personal records and files
_____Keep your tax information up to date
_____Keep your expense statements up to date
_____Do one job you have put off for over a year
_____Before the day is over, select a piece of mind
food and get started reading or listening

SCRIPTURE REFERENCES TO SELF-IMAGE

"For you are a holy people, dedicated to the Lord your God. He has chosen you from all the people on the face of the whole earth to be his own chosen ones" (Deuteronomy 7:6).

"Thank you for making me so wonderfully complex! It is amazing to think about. Your workmanship is marvelous—and how well I know it" (Psalm 139:14).

"For long ago the Lord had said to Israel: I have loved you, O my people, with an everlasting love; with lovingkindness I have drawn you to me" (Jeremiah 31:3).

"We should not be like cringing, fearful slaves, but we should behave like God's very own children, adopted into the bosom of his family, and calling to him, 'Father, Father'" (Romans 8:15).

"And I am sure that God who began the good work within you will keep right on helping you grow in his grace until his task within you is finally finished on that day when Jesus Christ returns" (Philippians 1:6).

"For you have been chosen by God himself—you are priests of the King, you are holy and pure, you are God's very own —all this so that you may show to others how God called you out of the darkness into his wonderful light" (1 Peter 2:9).

FAMILIAR QUOTATIONS ABOUT SELF-IMAGE

"When you're through changing, you're through."—Bruce Barton

"Self-confidence, in itself, is of no value. It is useful only when put to work."—Anonymous

"Everybody is ignorant—only on different subjects."—Will Rogers

"Success is more attitude than aptitude."—Anonymous

"In order to appreciate excellence you must yourself have struggled for it."—Anonymous

"Keep away from people who try to belittle your ambitions. Small people always do that, but the really great make you feel that you, too, can become great."—Mark Twain

"I could live a week on one good compliment."—Mark Twain

"The Lord can't use unscarred people. A dusty Bible leads to a dirty life."—Anonymous

"A man was applying for a job of private secretary to Winston Churchill. Before introducing him, an aunt of Churchill's told the man: 'Remember, you will see all of Winston's faults in the first five hours. It will take you a lifetime to discover his virtues.'"—Anonymous source

"True friends don't coddle your weaknesses; they encourage your strengths."—Anonymous

"A little daily dose of success is enough to keep most of us going."—Anonymous

"The man who does not read good books has no advantage over the man who can't read them."—Mark Twain

"Do what you can, with what you have, where you are."—Teddy Roosevelt

PART TWO
HOW TO SET AND ATTAIN PERSONAL AND FAMILY GOALS

5 / Think Big, Raise Elephants

As we begin to consider goal setting, let us allow ourselves to get into a "no limitations" mind-set. Achievers do not put limits on themselves.

ALL HIGH ACHIEVERS ARE
GOAL-ORIENTED PEOPLE

Other people settle for a picnic when God wants to give them a banquet. High achievers don't settle for less than the best. We must always be willing to have outrageous results. Ovid once said, "God gave man an upright countenance to survey the heavens and to look upward towards the stars."

Most high achievers have certain things in common. Fifty percent of the people who are doctors choose this profession as a goal by the time they reach age twelve. I have friends in the Chicago area. One son in this family is an outstanding heart surgeon. His mother told me that he decided at three years of age that he wanted to be a doctor and never changed his mind.

In goal-oriented people there is a concentration of ability, effort, and energy toward achieving an objective. Living with goals brings focus into one's life.

General Douglas MacArthur made a memorable statement as he left the Philippines in retreat. "I shall return," were his parting words. As he sped away in the PT boat which plowed through the waves to take him and his family to safety, General MacArthur was already laying plans to fulfill that goal. From that moment on, the waking hours of his day were spent exercising an army, resurrecting a navy, securing an air force, mobilizing a nation to do one thing—to return him to the place he had left. That is what goal-orientation will do for a person.

The Word of God is replete with men and women who were goal-oriented. Moses, for example, did not seem to get his life into focus until he was eighty years old. You are never too old to set goals. After arguing with God for a long time, Moses finally understood that God was going to use him to organize the Israelite slaves being held in bondage out of Egypt, free them, and march them across the desert to the promised land. Forty years later, the job was done. In the meantime, when his wife and father-in-law turned against him, Moses was not side-tracked from the goal. Even Aaron, his right-hand man and spokesman, turned against him, but Moses did not lose his focus. Finally all the people turned on him while he was on Mount Sinai, but Moses stood firm for God and the goal. History and the Word of God tell us he got the job done.

It seems significant that my son, when he was twelve years old, believed God gave him the goal to attend the Air Force Academy. Setting that goal at age twelve gave purpose and focus to his life from that time until he reached the goal of being accepted.

Paul Meyer of Success Motivation Institute says, "What you ardently desire, sincerely believe in, vividly imagine, enthusiastically act on must inevitably come to pass." That statement is almost a paraphrase of Hebrews 11:1: "What is faith? It is the confident assurance that something we want is going to happen. It is the certainty that what we hope for is waiting for us, even though we cannot see it up ahead." Of course, those things that we ardently desire must also be the things we know to be God's will for us, which we will discuss later.

Abraham Lincoln must have had goal-orientation in mind when he said, "Things may come to those who wait . . . but only the things left over from those who hustle."

GOALS ARE BUILT AROUND A PURPOSE

Before we can set goals for anything—a business, a family, or a life—there needs to be a stated purpose. When the going gets rough, as you move towards the goal, you will find motivation to keep going if your purpose is well defined and sufficiently worthy.

I am continually amazed how many schools, churches, families, and individuals strive to set goals but have not bothered to state the purpose of the program. Every person needs to take the time to pray over and think through the purpose of his or her life. Only God knows ultimately what his purpose and plan for our lives really is, but we should come to some conclusions as to what we believe the purpose of our lives should be. That purpose needs to be written down and it should become a part of our focus.

It took me several weeks of thinking, off and on, to write my life's purpose. I wrote it and rewrote it until I was satisfied that it was what pleases God in regard to my life.

My statement reads: "The purpose of my life is to know God the Father through the person of his Son Jesus; to be in control of my life; to wed my abilities to God's opportunities and to use what comes of that union for the honor, the praise, and the glory of God."

Determine right now to write a purpose for your life. Take your time. Write something down. Let it sit for a day or two, come back to it, pray about it, then write it again. Put it away, come back to it, and continue the process until you are satisfied you have come to a satisfactory statement of your purpose for living.

Once you have defined purpose, I am convinced decision-making is easier. There are things I no longer pray about. If they are not in keeping with the purpose of my life I simply put them out of my mind. As an example, I walked on the campus of a college recently and as I walked past the chapel, the president was coming out the door. He saw me and said, "Thank God, you're here."

"What's wrong?" I asked.

"I have the 350 students sitting in the chapel and the speaker hasn't shown up. Could you share something with the students?" he asked.

"Of course," I replied.

The reason I said "yes" was because I have the ability to speak before groups and I had some insights that I was able to share. The opportunity had just been made available to me. And it was within the purpose of my life. There was no need to pray about it. I simply walked in and spoke with the students.

Now if I walked into a grade school and somebody asked me to speak to the students, I don't think I would say "yes" so quickly. I don't have the ability to speak well to younger students. I have a hard time communicating with children that age. Bring your whole class and we will go sailing on my boat and have a great time. Let me go out with them for recess and we will enjoy each other. I love children. But I do not have the ability to speak to them in a group, to hold their attention, and to make it a meaningful meeting. In fact, I am so bad at it that if I accepted such an appointment I wouldn't sleep well for several nights before or after. Since I settled on the purpose of my life, I no longer feel guilty for not taking such engagements. An opportunity may be afforded, but if I don't have the ability to perform so that God is honored and glorified, then I simply turn it down.

To put it bluntly, if you have a good singing voice, and your purpose is to glorify God with your singing, then when someone offers you a job in a steel mill, you probably shouldn't take it, for if you took the noisy mill job it would possibly destroy your ear for music.

WHAT IS A GOAL?

I have been a goal setter for years. Many books have been written on the subject, and there are probably as many definitions of a goal as there are writers and speakers on the subject. I have not been fully satisfied with any definition I have found, so I made up my own. Like the preacher, who wrote his own commentary so he would have at least one with which to agree, I wrote my own definition. *A goal is the end to which a plan takes a person.* If one doesn't have a plan he doesn't have a goal. You might have a thought or an idea, but without a plan you don't have a goal. Sometimes people talk about their vision or their dreams. All too often I have watched dreams turn into nightmares. If the dreams had led to plans, the plans could have led to goals and the nightmares might have been avoided.

I developed my definition from watching some of those visionaries' dreams turn into nightmares. Since 1964 I have been involved in fund-raising activities for many Christian organizations. Fund raising is interesting. I usually am not with a group long before the organization's skeletons start popping out of the closets. When they do, I find some of the most interesting events that have taken place in the name of some lofty vision which was called a "goal," but which had no plan. The Scriptures teach us, "We should have plans—counting on God to direct us" (Proverbs 16:9).

The theme of my Planned Living Seminars, and I suppose of my life, is Proverbs 24:3, 4: "Any enterprise is built by wise planning, becomes strong through common sense, and profits wonderfully by keeping abreast of the facts."

One of the main reasons that goal setters are high achievers is because real goal setters make plans to meet the goal. If you have been one who has set goals and have not met them, chances are you either didn't plan or else you did not understand how to put together a proper plan. In this section we are going through a step-by-step procedure on how to set a goal and how to make a plan to attain that goal.

6 / Where to Set Goals

It is amazing to me how many people are able to set goals for their businesses or in their corporate position but have never considered setting goals in their personal and family lives.

An official of the Boeing Corporation attended a seminar I was teaching in Seattle. Later he told his pastor, "I do goal setting all the time at work, but I never thought of setting spiritual goals for myself."

GOALS SHOULD BE SET IN SIX AREAS

Companies will spend thousands of dollars to send their personnel to seminars, put them up in hotels for three days or a week, hoping they will learn something about goal setting. Yet the same man who orders that seminar held for his people does not take the time to teach his child to be goal-oriented. Then one day when that child is ready to enter college or the work force and someone asks him what he wants to do he doesn't know.

When our country was rural and most businesses were home businesses, such as the village blacksmith shop, the children learned by working with their parents, whose goal setting and achievement process were simply a part of their life as well. Today parents arise early, put on their work clothes, business suits, or overalls, leave the house, and go somewhere to work. In all my years of growing up, or as an adult, I never saw the place my father worked or knew exactly what he did. He worked in a paper mill. I am told he was a good, skillful worker, but I never saw him on the job.

My oldest son David is goal-oriented. All across the country we hear that young people will never be able to buy homes. I don't believe that. David and his wife Arlene were married in December of 1980. They spent part of their honeymoon in their own condominium. Separately, before they met, they each had the goal of owning their own home. They were working toward that goal. They pooled their goals and their resources and at age nineteen and twenty-one they were married and moved into their own $60,000 home.

Goal setting orients and helps pay the price of achievement. We must not allow our minds to be limited by what others are saying.

SPIRITUAL GOALS

Every person needs to set annual spiritual goals. Most people don't grow because they don't plan to grow. For too long some have gone to church, listened, and expected spiritual growth to take place which would solve their problems.

I'm convinced most people want to grow spiritually but they have not grasped the concept that it can happen anytime they begin to plan for spiritual growth.

The person who expects nothing is seldom disappointed. The trouble with doing nothing is that one never knows when he is finished.

Some people operate on the calendar year, from January 1 through December 31. Others function on a fiscal year, which might be from July 1 through June 30. Others relate their activities to the school year—September through early June, with the rest of the summer thrown in for bedlam with the children home from school. I happen to operate on the vacation year, with the new year beginning after our annual vacation.

We usually try to take our vacation the latter part of July or the first of August when the weather is quite good for sailing in the northwest. All during the year I keep tossing notes and scraps of information into a file—things I want to do in the coming year. As I sail, I let my mind work through the coming year, and by the time vacation is over, I'm committed to my goals for the next twelve months.

My spiritual goal this past year was to make friends with two ungodly, cursing, reprobate people. For some time I have felt myself becoming too surrounded by people who believe everything I believe. In Christian work it is easy to isolate ourselves from the very people we ought to be reaching.

Perhaps we need to set a spiritual goal of studying prophecy for a year or learning a new method of Bible study. It could well be that we should spend this year learning what prayer is all about and practicing how to do it.

We should be serious about our Christian lives. Maybe this is the year we should give to ministering to several new families in our church. We might plan to have them to dinner, or have them join us on a picnic, or take them to a ball game.

I can't begin to imagine what our churches would be like if we as individual members began to set spiritual goals on an annual basis. Remember, when you set the goal you must have a plan. Later in this section we will see exactly how to set and attain goals.

SOCIAL GOALS

If you have been invited to someone's home during the last thirty or sixty days, it was probably because they planned to have you over. When you have someone in for a dinner party it is the result of your planning to do so.

As a pastor I have many times heard things like, ''Pastor,

I am so discouraged. We never go anywhere. My husband doesn't take me to dinner. We don't have anybody over. We never go to anyone else's house.'' We should understand that those things don't just happen. Someone plans for them to happen. People who have friends work at being friendly.

Why not set a goal of becoming friends with a retired person? There is much to be learned from their years of experience, which could also fit in with our spiritual goals if we work it right.

My wife and I had an unusual courtship while we were both working at the same Bible conference. Before the summer was over we were engaged, and before the year was over, we were married. Consequently we did not know each other very well when we began to live together.

You can't imagine how stunned I was to learn she liked opera. Me? I liked the Grand Ole Opry. Part of our social goals have been to attend some of the things my wife enjoys. Married couples should ask if their spouse has unfulfilled social desires, some places they have always wanted to go. Couples should talk it over and set some social goals.

It might be even more important for single people to set social goals than married people. Too many times single people withdraw into a world all their own. This need not happen if they are willing to set some goals. The standard saying in the world of goal setters is, ''Plan your work and work your plan.''

FAMILY GOALS

A question I often ask families with children is concerning their parenting goals. What are they trying to accomplish with their children? Many people today seem to feel that if they provide a house to live in, clothes to wear, a school to learn, food to eat, and Little League for fun, that they are parenting. This is called provisioning, but not necessarily parenting.

Parenting is preparing a child to become a mature adult.

Parenting is making the effort to see that a child understands what self-discipline is and how to exercise it. So many times we see the verse quoted: "Teach a child to choose the right path, and when he is older he will remain upon it" (Proverbs 22:6). The sense of the verse to me is that if the child is taught to discipline himself to be obedient to parents, then he will self-discipline himself to be, when he is an adult, obedient to God.

The greatest disservice a parent can do to his children is to fail to teach them self-discipline. Children may know a hundred Scripture verses but what good are they if they aren't self-disciplined enough to apply them?

Very early in our marriage, Mary and I set three goals in the parenting process. We have two boys. We knew that one day they would have to become men in their own right, husbands in their own right, and most likely, fathers as well. In order for them to accomplish this, we felt certain things had to take place. First, they needed to learn to be independent of us. They could never become their own person before God and man if they were hanging onto us. Second, they needed to learn to be dependent upon God. In time and in eternity we need God, and our children must understand this also. Finally, they would always have to accept the responsibility for their own actions. They could not be allowed to rationalize, spiritualize, or in any other way, cop out of responsibility. When they were wrong they had to confront it and admit it.

This is not a book on child rearing or how to teach children to set goals. That might be my next book and seminar. But if you want a child to accept the responsibility of his actions, to say "I am sorry," to ask forgiveness, then you had better be willing to do the same. Some of the best moments of teaching have been when I have had to tell my boys, "I am sorry; I was wrong. Please forgive me."

As we think through our family goals, we should ask ourselves what kinds of recreation or vacation can be done that will help accomplish these goals. We should carefully think through our children's work schedule and see if what they are doing is really building something into them or if they are simply doing busy work so we feel good and fool ourselves into thinking we are teaching them something.

Our children are tougher and more capable than most of us give them credit for being. Often I have reminded myself that one of the longest rides by a pony express mail carrier was done by William Cody, known as Buffalo Bill. He was fifteen years old at the time.

To set family and parenting goals means we will need to place confidence in our spouse and our children. David, at age fifteen, took his mother (who is great for responsibilities below deck, but didn't know much about sailing at the time), his thirteen-year-old brother, and a family of four to Victoria, Canada. They boarded our boat, at that time a thirty-eight-foot sailing ketch, and sailed from our home in Seattle, up Puget Sound, across the Straits of San Juan de Fuca to Victoria, and then through the San Juan Islands on the way home. During that week's cruise, David was skipper of the boat, handled the navigation, and was in complete charge. I was on a business trip.

Frankly, the boat cost me more than our house, but I let him go, because I wanted him to learn to be independent of us, dependent upon God, and responsible for his own actions. How else was he going to learn if we didn't let him try? There was a lot of training that led up to his being able to do this. Children can be our greatest joy and the toughest assignment we may ever have in life, but worth every effort when things turn out well.

FINANCIAL GOALS

Every person and every family needs financial goals. If it were a commitment of every American to take care of himself now and in the future, our nation would not be in some of the social and economic struggles we face today. Being independent is not everyone's goal as it once was. There are people today, and more than a few, who want somebody to take care of them. This may be the result of parents not teaching them to take care of themselves.

If we don't make financial plans for ourselves, no one else will. One time in a meeting a believer told me, "But God takes care of the lilies and the sparrows. Won't he take care of us?"

Of course. That is why God has provided seasons for planting and harvesting, and the rain to make things grow. What God said to Adam is for us today as well: "And to Adam, God said, 'Because you listened to your wife and ate the fruit when I told you not to, I have placed a curse upon the soil. All your life you will struggle to extract a living from it. It will grow thorns and thistles for you, and you shall eat its grasses. All your life you will sweat to master it, until your dying day'" (Genesis 3:17).

I like Billy Sunday's practical theology. "Don't pray for a house unless you want to pick up a saw and hammer and start cutting boards and driving nails," he once said.

It is not sinful to lay financial plans or any other kind of plans for the future. We have not thwarted the Spirit of God because we have a plan. He can influence us to move in another direction any time he wants. If we are moving in a direction that he doesn't like, then he can correct the course, a maneuver which is always easier when the object to be steered is already in motion.

Solomon wisely spoke concerning work: "Take a lesson from the ants, you lazy fellow. Learn from their ways and be wise! For though they have no king to make them work, yet they labor hard all summer, gathering food for the winter. But you—all you do is sleep. When will you wake up? 'Let me sleep a little longer!' Sure, just a little more! And as you sleep, poverty creeps upon you like a robber and destroys you; want attacks you in full armor" (Proverbs 6:6-10).

We had two children when I pastored in Nampa, Idaho. We received $238 per month and lived in two large Sunday school rooms. I was a spiritual man. Pastoring in Vancouver, Washington, the salary started at $500 per month with no benefits, no insurance, no car allowance, no housing allowance—nothing extra. I was a spiritual man then, too. In each place I started a small business on the side and spoke everywhere I could for whatever people would give me just to keep food on the table and clothes on the kids. I was a spiritual man.

Today, I own an older home on Lake Washington, live aboard my forty-eight-foot sailing ketch, drive a decent car, and dress comfortably and correctly. I am still a spiritual man. I have been spiritual with nothing, and I have been spiritual with something. The only difference is that it is more enjoyable to be spiritual with a little something than with nothing. The difference has been planning.

The key for our family financially is not how much we make, but what we do with what we make, as we will discuss more fully when we come to the section on budgeting. Right now we must simply accept the statement as a fact and understand that the setting of financial goals will assure our future. Remember, "A goal is the end to which a plan takes a person." So we must be willing to lay solid plans for our future.

Our financial goals and our family goals might walk hand in hand. If we have always wanted to take our family on a tour of the historical sites in the east, or to Europe, the Holy Land, or Africa, we must simply begin a financial plan that will lead us to that goal.

At one point in my ministry I was attempting to help an ex-convict restructure his life. We were talking about his future and he said, "This would all be so easy if I were like you and had a home, a nice wife, a good job, and children."

I bristled, "Why do you think I have those? Where do you think they came from? Nobody gave them to me," I said. "They are the result of making plans and working hard."

Our potential for financial stability and security will double, triple, and more if we begin to plan for it. Believe me, I have seen it happen for me and scores of others. People don't secure their families' future by accident. They set goals and make plans.

As we set financial goals, we must get in the habit of making a complete financial statement at least once each year. How else will we know if we are gaining or losing?

Material things are not sinful. People do sinful things with them. The lust for things is sinful and problematic. One of the rules I set for myself early in marriage and parenting was never to get upset about something happening to some material possessions. It can always be fixed or replaced with money. Remember what Billy Sunday said, "Money—you can't take it with you, and if you could it might burn."

Mary and I have had our home burned. The kids have damaged the boats. All of us have had automobile accidents. So what, as long as nobody is hurt? It can all be fixed. So why get excited?

It is all right to have financial goals, so we must be willing when we start listing goals to admit where we would like to be financially as we look at the future.

The Lord's return may be imminent. But that does not exempt us from making plans. We must set goals, plan, and work as if we will be here a lifetime and yet live as if this is our last day.

MENTAL GOALS

What is it that we are planning to learn this year? Why not go back to college in the evening to take some courses? We should stay on the cutting edge of learning.

Perhaps there are some classic pieces of literature we feel we could benefit by reading. The classics should be a part of our lives. We should consider making a reading list and then working our way through perhaps two books per year. This can be where mind food comes into plan in our goal setting as we begin to plan our living.

I am almost completely devoid of mechanical skills and knowledge. One of my learning goals is to learn how to care properly for the ancient diesel engine which is an auxiliary in my sailboat.

We might better ourselves at our jobs if we were to follow

some course of study. One of the men I discipled in Seattle was a fine warehouse worker for a major department store. It was a thrill to have him one day announce he was going to discipline himself and take some additional college classes so he could move on into management. In every way he will be a broader and better person for making the effort to involve himself in the learning process.

We must turn off the TV and start learning. We must become a participant, not just a spectator. We can do it!

PHYSICAL GOALS

We all need some physical goals. We all need to get in shape and stay in shape. What do we want to accomplish this year in our weight control program? How about an exercise program—jogging, walking, or whatever? If we can't find anything else to do, then we might play golf. I tried to learn, but soon came to the conclusion that I did not need to pay money to get frustrated. I can do that for nothing. As part of our physical goals, we should give some attention in our lives for recreation. Vance Havner said, "Come apart, before you come apart." Jesus took his disciples away from the crowds from time to time. "Then Jesus suggested 'Let's get away from the crowds for a while and rest.' For so many people were coming and going that they scarcely had time to eat. So they left by boat for a quieter spot" (Mark 6:31, 32).

People who do sedentary work especially need the mental and emotional release that physical involvement can give them. We are all in need of some type of getting away. We should not feel guilty about it. Because it is necessary to our lifetime goals, we should feel good about taking time away from work for relaxation.

We will work harder, perform better, be more patient, and generally improve our disposition and our life in general if we take care of our weight, exercise, and slip out of the system for a few hours and on occasion for a few days.

We perhaps ought to plan something physical to do as a

family. I said plan, because I underscore again, "A goal is the end to which a plan takes a person." If we don't plan it, it probably won't happen.

Occasionally in my Planned Living Seminars, someone will remark, "I don't want to get *that* organized. I won't have any free time." There is no such thing as free time. You always exchange it for something—probably TV.

7 / How to Set Goals

Setting goals is not a mystery. It is like every other worth-while thing—it takes some effort. But since we are going to be alive and walking the earth for quite a while yet, we should begin now to do something to make the rest of the time count for something worthwhile.

TAKE ACTION

The first thing we must realize is that nobody can set goals for us. Others may be a sounding board. There is a benefit in wise counsel and having someone on whom to try out ideas, but in the final analysis, we must set our own goals.

In counseling others, I often find those who want to have someone tell them what their goals should be. If we have never set goals before then we must start by starting. I've often said that my mind goes into gear when my pen hits the paper. We might start that way—by getting out a clean sheet of paper. We might start by listing some of the goals we might want to set for ourselves, paying little attention to priority or order at this time. Then we should start praying over them and considering them in the light of the following goal-setting steps.

WRITE THEM DOWN

A goal is not a goal until it is written down. Up until that time we may call it a goal but it is only a thought, a consideration, a concept, or a dream. For an idea to become a goal it must be written so it is projected outside ourselves.

Once we have written it down, we are able to visualize it and begin to lay the plans as to how we are going to attain it. For example, we may have the best voice in the world, but unless we develop a plan as to how to develop it, the goal of being an accomplished singer will never be attained. As long as the goal is buried in our minds and hearts we can fool ourselves into thinking we have a goal. But until it is objectified in writing, it probably will never be developed.

We could bury $10,000 in the ground and keep telling ourselves that one day we are going to take it and turn it into a million dollars. We can be smug about it. We may even tell others that we are already worth a million dollars because of what we have said we are going to do with the money. However, it is a fact that until we take the money out of the ground and start to work with it, it will never produce anything for us. The same is true of an idea inside of us. It may be a worthy idea, but it won't become anything until we write it down and turn it into a goal.

BE WILLING TO GROW

For years I used to drive by an old Burma Shave sign in Idaho. It read, "Don't be afraid. Play your hunch. Be top banana, not one of the bunch." One of the greatest things about goal setting is that when it is done right, it will keep us growing.

Our goal must have "God room" in it. By that I mean provision must be allowed for God to make us mature and to stretch us as we work toward attaining the goal. The Lord has his hand on us for a continual process of growth. In our goal setting we must give him a chance to make us grow.

We shouldn't excuse ourselves from goal setting by asking, "What if I set the wrong goal?" If we do have the wrong goal or an unreasonable goal we can change it, as we will see at the end of this section. For now we must determine to lay aside our rationalization for not having set goals before and get busy with pencil and paper.

Allowing "God room" means we must make good goals. A goal is not a good one if when we write it down we know for certain we can do it without effort. On the other hand, a goal is not a good goal if it is filled with foolish, unreasonable expectations. We must be realistic and, at the same time, we must include an element of faith so we are always reaching for new victories.

When Sir Francis Chichester sailed around the world alone in a fifty-six-foot yawl, he did so at an age when most men are ready to retire. Sir Francis spoke the truth when he said, "The thrill is in the journey, the hardship, not in tying up at the dock."

We must keep reaching, keep stretching, keep trying. Our lives carry with them an excitement and motivation when we set goals with "God room." We must strive to go beyond what we know we can accomplish.

REMEMBER THE PURPOSE

To be a good goal, the goal must always be within the stated purpose of our lives. I can't imagine why a person would want to set a goal that is outside of his purpose. Remember, we are going to be spending time building plans to reach these goals, so we must set our wills not to waste our time with things that are outside the stated purpose.

For years I watched people who I felt had less ability than I accomplish more than I did. Finally I noticed they were often doing only one or two things whereas I was running here and there doing a little bit of this and a little bit of that. I used to say in jest, "I'm losing a little on every deal and making it up on the volume."

Often I have said to my wife, "I have too many strings on

my guitar." My mother used to say, "Lanson, you have too many irons in the fire." Setting goals within our purpose will keep us focused. We should all strive to do a few things well and not dissipate our energies doing things that don't fit our overall life goals or things that others can do better.

NOW START WRITING

Once we thoroughly understand these first four steps, then we must actually write out some goals. For the sake of illustration, let us see what my son had for goals during his sophomore year of high school. He was fifteen years old the September he put together this set of goals for himself:

GOALS TO ATTEND THE AIR FORCE ACADEMY

Spiritual: Work on my personal witness (musical taste, language, and actions). Help someone get straightened out.

Mental: Keep semester one grade point at 3.71 or above. Semester two at 3.85 or above. Monday, Wednesday, Friday I will study at the library from 7 to 9 P.M. during wrestling season. Friday may be exchanged for Thursday if I want to boogie [for readers my age, that means go out and have fun]. I will keep up or ahead on all long-range assignments.

Physical: Get myself and everyone on the team in great shape. I will learn the arm drags, David's switch, and John's stack series. I will keep a good attitude about myself and the sport, but will keep up the grades.

Financial: I will work five out of eight Saturdays. Three out of eight Saturdays I will ski, dive, or date. (Check into getting out of school for skiing.) On Saturdays, I will work at least five hours for $20. After wrestling season, I will work three hours a night, every Tuesday and Thursday, till school is out. After that, I will work five hours a day, five days a week, till I leave on my trip.

Recreation: Ski whenever possible. Buy a canoe or kayak, go diving often, ride my bike to and from school, weather permitting. Go on a date once a month (or more). After wrestling, get in forty-five minutes of truly solid drum practice.

Planning: Make out a weekly list of things for myself to do (be specific as to time allowed and what will be accomplished) and stick to it.

If a fifteen-year-old boy can set goals and make plans then any of us can do it.

SEVEN STEPS TO PLANNING

The next seven steps are the core issues involved in making plans to meet a goal.

1. List two problems connected with meeting this goal—the difficulties, the things blocking the way. These are the issues we must deal with as we build our plans.

2. List at least two solutions for each of these problems. There is always something we can do about a problem. One of the things I like about cruising in my sailboat is that I am on my own. When I am away from people I must be resourceful enough to be self-reliant. I learned a long time ago that I could break some gear, run aground, lose an anchor, or spring a leak. But there is always something I can do about each problem if I take my brain out of neutral and come up with the solution to the problem I had already anticipated.

3. List two benefits we will receive from achieving this goal. If it does not benefit us then we will not accomplish it. To be an achiever there has to be some benefit in it for us. I am not talking just about material things. There are many

benefits in life that go far beyond those. For instance, a great benefit is the respect of others, or even our self-respect, when we finally break that habit which has been bugging us. We may benefit from the joy of helping others once we have reached some particular goal. We must not wear that sanctified spiritual veneer which causes us to say, "I'm not interested in benefits for myself." Of course we are, and it is a good thing we are or we might not be enjoying the benefit of eternal life.

4. Now comes the tough one. We should ask if there is anyone with whom we should share this goal, or should we keep it to ourselves. Not every goal should be shared. Sometimes people feel if they tell everyone what they hope to do that by doing so they will put themselves under enough pressure to follow through to accomplish the goal.

When we share a goal with someone it becomes an expectation they place upon us, which can be bad. For instance, I don't mind telling someone that at one time I weighed 255 pounds and that today I am down to 216. But I would not tell them what I hope to weigh as a goal because I don't want them to ask me how I am doing on my weight control. If I am not doing too well at that time, then I won't have to listen to their negative input.

Also to tell others about some goal we have set makes it difficult for us to revise that goal should it prove impractical or unwise. To save face we might try to hang onto it long after we should have abandoned it.

5. Make a list of the things that must be given up in order to accomplish the goal. This step separates those who do things from those who hope to do things. Sidney Howard said, "One half of knowing what you want is knowing what you must give up in order to get it."

I know exactly what I must give up if I am going to lose weight. I must omit bread, potatoes with gravy, bread, a bowl of buttered popcorn each night, and bread. When I do, the weight begins to fall.

It fascinates me to meet people who pay to go to group

meetings to help them lose weight. I never met anyone who did not know that the way to lose weight was to eat fewer calories than he burned. But some people seem to need the encouragement and advice others can give them to make weight loss as painless as possible. Whatever method a person uses, there will always be a price to pay, a personal sacrifice, to achieve any worthwhile goal.

Whatever our goal is as it has been written, we should think carefully about what we must lay aside, what we give up in order to get to the goal. Jesus spoke about a price to be paid. "Remember, I don't even own a place to lay my head. Foxes have dens to live in, and birds have nests, but I, the Messiah, have no earthly home at all" (Luke 9:58). To follow him meant that some of them would have to give up some things.

To build a good marriage we give up certain things. To be a good parent we give up certain things. To reach any goal there are some things we must give up. Listing those things to be exchanged for our goals is part of the process in making the plan to reach goals.

6. We must answer the question as to whether or not we are willing to give up those things. It does no good to identify the problem unless we are going to do something about it. Goal setting sooner or later gets down to the setting of our will in self-discipline to do what must be done.

No person can do everything, so we must decide what it is we are going to do and what we are going to do without. If we choose not to answer this question in the affirmative, then we shouldn't blame God or anyone else about our lack of accomplishments. High achievers are goal-oriented people and goal-oriented people are willing to lay things aside to reach their objective.

7. Ask, "Is accomplishing this goal satisfying?" If there is not satisfaction in it then we probably won't carry it to completion. There is no trophy, monetary prize, anything that can reward us like knowing we have done our best and that we are satisfied with the result.

DIVIDE GOALS INTO PIECES

Once the seven steps just stated have been carefully fulfilled, we next divide the goal into manageable pieces, definable steps along the way to completion of the goal. For example, a runner must decide whether he wants to participate in the Olympic marathon. If he does he won't begin by running twenty-six miles for a couple of times and show up at the Olympics. He trains; he gets himself a coach. He sets up a training program and timetable. He runs in local races, then regionals. National and international competitions are necessary to get the invitation to the Olympic finals. Somewhere in all of this preparation is a defined goal ahead for which all the plans lead. The goal is the culmination of many decisions, large and small, that affect his work, his family, his recreation—everything about his life.

Financial goals are always easy to divide into pieces because the dollar amounts can be objectively defined. A person who wants to get out of debt can plan to reduce the debt by a certain amount each month. It is easy to see at any time whether he is keeping to his plan. A savings plan is much the same. A goal to increase an investments portfolio may be planned in much the same way. But someone who is in debt for $2000 will not suddenly get out of debt unless he comes up with a workable plan, such as setting aside $100 a month for twenty months.

Someone who plans to be a millionaire, if that is what he believes Gods wants him to do, must plan how much he will be worth by a certain time. The large goal becomes many small steps within the plan.

SET THE PRIORITY ON THE PIECES

We cannot be a goal setter without putting ourselves under some pressure. We must decide what we are going to do first, second, next, and so on. Then we must put a date beside each step so we have some way to measure how we are doing.

	Short Range (Less than 12 months)	Mid Range (12-36 months)	Long Range (Over 36 months)	How I feel about my progress (Annual Report)
		Date Accomplished	Date Accomplished	Date Accomplished
SPIRITUAL 1. 2. 3.				
FINANCIAL 1. 2. 3.				
MENTAL 1. 2. 3.				
SOCIAL 1. 2. 3.				
FOR MY FAMILY 1. 2. 3.				
PHYSICAL CONDITION 1. 2. 3.				

TURN THE GOAL INTO PROJECTS

There must be specific things we are going to do if we are to accomplish this goal. This will involve the day-to-day list of things to be done. For some this will be the schedule we make for ourselves on a particular day. Such a schedule will include activities we have planned to achieve the long range goal. For instance, in the case of my son's plan, he decided to spend two hours in the library during wrestling season. Therefore on Wednesday his daily schedule calls for going to the library at 7 P.M. and staying until 9 P.M. That was his project for that evening.

On the following page is one form of a goal layout sheet. We might enlarge it on our own paper or simply use a sheet of blank paper and follow through on the steps presented in this chapter. We shouldn't be fussy about the form it takes. The important thing is to have the foresight to make a plan and stick to it. One of my favorite mottos is "Do it now!"

8 / What If I Don't Make the Goal?

It would be nice if we were able to do everything we set out to do in life, but that is not going to happen. There are yet a couple of unanswered questions we must consider.

WHEN IS A GOAL SIMPLY A PIPE DREAM?

A goal is a pipe dream unless it affects our choices today. To put it another way, we will never achieve a goal in the future unless the future goal influences the choices we are making in the present. For example, if I am serious about losing weight and at some time in the future weighing less than I do now, then that goal must be lived out in today's meals. I must choose to eat less. To reach a goal we must monitor what we do daily or we will not reach the goal up ahead. If I don't consider my long-term goal when I sit down to eat my next meal, at that moment my goal has become a pipe dream. No amount of talking about it, writing about it, or praying over it will change it from a pipe dream back into a goal until I choose once again to allow it to affect my choices.

If my goal were to sail around the world, many things would have to happen. First I would write it down and put a time beside it. For example, my goal is in five years to sail around the world.

Next I would list all the problems and their solutions. For instance, I would have to get the boat ready. *Rogue* would need new fastenings, new standing rigging, new running rigging and the engine should be rebuilt. I could not go without one full set of sails plus a storm sail and additional downwind sails. For safety I would need to add a depth finder, a single side band radio, a VHF radio, and at least a radio direction finder.

I have just started with all of that but now I have to get myself in readiness. Navigation needs to be studied and learned. A course in diesel mechanics would be a must. Right now I know nothing about diesel engines. I will also have to be in top shape physically. Also I should do some study about weather and read up on sailing in a storm.

No, I'm not done. Then the route must be studied and the books and charts necessary to plot a safe passage will have to be purchased and pored over.

Perhaps I have worked on this for three and a half years. Eighteen months from sailing I walk through the local shopping mall. In the window of the local House of Leather is a sign, "Sale." I casually stroll in and look around. There are leather jackets and coats everywhere, but one catches my eye. Oh, oh. It is my size! I try it on and stand in front of the mirror. Man, do I look good! I have always wanted a coat like this—and think of the money I could save. After all, it is on sale.

If I give in to my urge to buy it, then my goal to sail around the world has turned into a pipe dream for that moment. Put enough of those moments together and I will not meet the goal. The reason is simple. There is no way that coat is going to help me reach the goal of sailing around the world. I should not be buying more things; I should be getting rid of things. In eighteen months my schedule calls for me to leave. I couldn't take the coat with me. If I put it below deck and left it the coat would mildew and rot. If I wore it on deck it would be ruined as soon as the salt water waves began to hit it. No matter how badly I want the coat or how good a buy it is, I must choose not to purchase it—that is, if I am to continue my goal as a real goal.

WHAT DO I DO IF I DON'T ACHIEVE THE GOAL?

Not every goal will be accomplished. Frankly, not every goal should be met. You may get moving toward a goal and find for one reason or another that it is no longer a valid or good goal. Your health might break. The economy might turn. God might suggest something different. Remember that Paul had his plans laid when he had a vision. "That night Paul had a vision. In his dream he saw a man over in Macedonia, Greece, pleading with him, 'Come over here and help us'" (Acts 16:9).

On more than one occasion I have been involved in a plan to attain a goal only to discover the goal was not a worthy one and I had to terminate the pursuit.

What should we do if we see a goal can't be reached? The answer is at some point in time we choose to stop our pursuit and move toward a new goal. One of the keys to being a successful goal setter is to control our ego and be willing to terminate the pursuit of a goal when the time is right. We must never say, "I can't do it. I quit." Don't even verbalize that. Rather, when we see the goal is not going to be reached, cannot be reached, or should not be reached, we must then choose the time, terminate the plan, and choose to move into another plan toward a new goal.

I have watched goal setting become a destructive thing in people's lives. Some of the companies who market through home businesses have at times been guilty of encouraging their sales people to set what are unrealistic goals. If a person struggling with a weak self-image is trying to break out of his shell, so to speak, but has set unrealistic goals he is consistently missing, his failure tends to reinforce his already poor self-image. What should be a good positive project has then become a negative force in his life. The only answer I know is to choose to go a new direction, but never quit trying.

MAKE SOME LISTS

Make lists of things you might consider undertaking. Consider the following headings:

Things I would like to start doing
Things I want to change
Things I want for my home
Spiritual things I want to know
Things I would like to stop doing
Places I want to go
Things I would like to be

SCRIPTURE REFERENCES TO GOAL SETTING

"Commit everything you do to the Lord. Trust him to help you do it and he will" (Psalm 37:5).

"Determination to be wise is the first step toward becoming wise! And with your wisdom, develop common sense and good judgment" (Proverbs 4:7).

"Hard work means prosperity; only a fool idles away his time" (Proverbs 12:11).

"We should make plans—counting on God to direct us" (Proverbs 16:9).

"If you love sleep, you will end in poverty. Stay awake, work hard, and there will be plenty to eat!" (Proverbs 20:13).

"No, dear brothers, I am still not all I should be but I am bringing all my energies to bear on this one thing: Forgetting the past and looking forward to what lies ahead, I strain to reach the end of the race and receive the prize for which God is calling us up to heaven because of what Christ Jesus did for us'' (Philippians 3:13, 14).

FAMILIAR QUOTATIONS ABOUT GOAL SETTING

''Goals serve as a stimulus to life. They tend to tap the deeper resources and draw out of life its best. Where there are no goals, neither will there be significant accomplishments. There will only be existence.''—Anonymous

''Following the path of least resistance is what makes men and rivers crooked. Men seldom drift to success.''
— Anonymous

''Every great achievement was once impossible.''
— Anonymous

''The difference between men consists, in great measure, in the intelligence of their observation. It is the close observation of little things which is the secret of success in business, in art, in science, and in every pursuit of life.''—Samuel Smiles

''A good follow-through is just as important in management as it is in bowling, tennis, or golf. Follow-through is the bridge between good planning and good results.''
— Anonymous

''Don't be afraid to take a big step if one is indicated. You can't cross a chasm in two small jumps.''—David Lloyd George

''Our problem is not the lack of knowing; it is the lack of doing. Most Christians *know* far more than they *do.*''—Mark Hatfield in *Conflict and Conscience.*

''You can't build a reputation on what you're going to do.''—Henry Ford

"Courage is doing what you're afraid to do. There can be no courage unless you're scared."—Eddie Rickenbacker

"The world belongs to the energetic."—Ralph Waldo Emerson

"Experience proves that most time is wasted, not in hours, but in minutes. A bucket with a small hole in the bottom gets just as empty as a bucket that is deliberately kicked over." — Paul J. Meyer

"Man's mind stretched by a new idea never goes back to its original dimensions."—Oliver Wendell Holmes

"Ever notice how your plans to lose weight always run into a snack?"—Anonymous

PART THREE
HOW TO MAKE
AND MAINTAIN
A PERSONAL
AND FAMILY
BUDGET

9 / Budget Your Way to Freedom

Many people seem to run out of money before they run out of month. People think that if they made more money they would be able to keep up financially. But the fact is that a person's financial future is usually more dependent on what he does with what he makes rather than simply increasing his income.

DON'T MISHANDLE WHAT YOU MAKE

While I was teaching my Planned Living Seminar in the midwest, a man came about twenty minutes late the first night. He sat six rows behind everyone else and at the end of the session he left before any of the others. I asked the pastor if he knew him. He replied that he had never seen him before. Later I learned that the man had come as the result of a newspaper article that grew out of an interview I had given earlier.

The next night I presented the step-by-step teaching of how to make a budget and how to stay on it. He was there with his wife, ten minutes early for the session. The next night he and his wife were on the front row taking careful notes in the manual.

After the meeting he came up and began to thank me for the instruction on budgeting. I asked him, "What do you do, sir?"

"I am a surgeon," he said. With this he looked to see if anyone was listening, and said, "I make over $125,000 per year and I couldn't tell you where $2,500 of it goes."

Believe me, it isn't how much a person makes that guarantees a secure future but what is done with it. All of us have known people who make $10,000 and spent $12,000. They change locations for jobs paying $13,500 but they spend $15,000. Then the wife goes to work and they then make $24,000 so they spend $26,000. Both get raises and make $27,000 and spend $30,000. Such people are always in trouble and have themselves convinced that they would be all right if they could just make a little more each month.

Having been a pastor for over twenty years, I have watched with interest people's reaction when I begin to talk to them about either making money or budgeting it. Some have actually asked me if I had laid my faith aside.

TALK ABOUT MONEY AND YOU CAN'T WIN

Run after money and you are materialistic.
Don't get it and you are looked on as a loser.
Get it and keep it and you are a miser.
Don't try to get it and you lack ambition.
Get money and spend it and you are a spendthrift.
Still have it at the end of your life and you are a fool;
　　you never had any fun with it.

Often I have said that I have chosen to talk and write about money because we need to be more careful with it because of the way the economy is going. The only thing that goes as far as it used to is a quarter when it falls to the floor and rolls under the bed. Someone said, "If your outgo exceeds your income, then your upkeep will be your downfall." We make many jokes about money, but it is time for all of us to get serious about the subject of budgeting.

WHY MY FAMILY BEGAN BUDGETING

Early in our marriage we had a good discussion about who was going to handle the finances. It was decided that Mary should bank the money, handle the checkbook, and pay the bills.

Puffed up from the positive stroke I ask, "How are we doing financially this month?"

She beams, "Just great. It is the twentieth of the month. I have all the bills paid, most of the groceries bought, and both cars are full of gas, and we have about $350 in the bank."

"Swell," I say. "Then it will be all right to take the boat radio in for repair? They thought it might cost about $125."

"Sure, honey, you have been working hard. It would be good for you to take a couple days and enjoy yourself," Mary said.

So I take the radio out, take it to the shop, go get it in a couple of days, and put it back on board the *Rogue*. The bill is $175 instead of $125, but most repairs usually are higher than the estimate. No big deal. We have been having a good month.

The next day I get on the plane and go on a three-day business trip. Mary meets me out front when I return to the airport and we start through the routine. She kisses me, sort of. By that time I sensed what we notice often. When our spouse seems to exude a certain atmosphere we are able to pick up through our pores that something is not quite right. Those vibrations seem to be coming from my wife. So I start in, "How are you? How are the boys? How's the dog? How is the boat?" Because I have always traveled considerably and was not home many times when bills were to be paid, it was logical that Mary could better keep track of such things. Also I learned early that I could make money and Mary could keep it. That seemed important. The real deciding factor was that I can't seem to add and subtract and she can. See how far I have come in my self-image? My male ego will now allow me to admit to the things I don't do well.

Our lives often went something like this. I would be gone

for eight days doing fund raising or preaching and Mary would meet me at the airport when I came in. She always waits in the car in front of the terminal. I hop in the car and give her a kiss. She hands me the important messages and phone calls. She drives. I glance over the material and then ask, "How are you, honey?"

"Fine."

"How are the boys?"

"They are fine."

"How's the dog?"

"Lady's fine," she would reply.

Now the important things. "Did the boat ride out the storm all right?"

"Yes, David and Lanny put on a couple of more lines. Those boys are so good around boats. You have really taught them well, honey."

To this point she is answering each one, "Fine and OK."

Then I ask, "How are we doing financially?"

Now she drops the bomb, "We've got a problem."

"What do you mean, a problem?" I ask.

"The day you left I got a bill for car insurance for $450 and it's due by the fifteenth of next month. I would have been able to pay it," she continues, "but you took all the money and fixed the radio in the boat." There is definitely an accusatory tone in her voice.

Now it starts—the argument. "What do you mean, I took the money? Three days ago when I was home we were in great shape. You told me so yourself. Didn't you know that bill was coming?" Now it was my time to be accusatory.

Mary's reply was, "I can't keep track of everything you are doing. You have so many tracks you are running on I don't see how you can keep them straight." (I couldn't. That was why I was running.) "What do you think? That I'm stealing your money or something? There is my purse. Take the checkbook out and look for yourself. Everything you make and everything spent is in the checkbook."

Then comes the closing shot. "If you don't like the way I

am doing things with the money, then do it yourself."

It would be nice if I could tell you that this happened only occasionally, but actually it was a rather frequent occurrence. Finally one day I said, "Mary, we are going to budget. The church budgets, the business budgets, and we are going to budget." I paused for effect, and I got it.

"No, we are not!" Mary shot back. "You get all these bright ideas, give them to me, and then you get on a plane and fly out of town and I'm left to follow through on all this stuff. I already have enough mess to keep track of. I'm not adding one more thing to it."

Well, we worked our way through that one and started budgeting. In this section I am going to explain exactly what my wife and I started to do and still do today. After we had been on the budget for about six weeks, I was in the living room reading. Mary came up behind me and kissed me on the neck and said, "Thank you, honey, for putting us on a budget. I feel so free."

I was surprised by her words: "I feel so free." Most often we think of a budget as a confining thing.

"There are no surprises anymore. I know where I am and what is happening. I'm in control of the circumstances," was her reply.

WHAT IS A BUDGET?

Once while I was riding on a plane, the man next to me asked me what I did. As I shared with him about the seminar I teach he said, "I'm on a budget."

"What's it like?" I asked him. He began to tell me that he knew what his car payment was, his house payment, insurance, that he had to pay heat, power, water, and about how much he spent on food per month. What he explained to me was not a budget—it was a guess.

According to the dictionary a budget is "a written statement of estimated income and expenses for a designated period of time."

PURPOSES OF A BUDGET

Budgets are made for three purposes.

1. *A budget is a tool for guidance.* Spending needs to be given some direction if it is going to be kept under control. People do not sit down once a year and say, ''How far can I get in the hole this year and how tough can I make it on myself and my family?'' But this does happen when we do impulse buying, buying on credit, or when we have no direction for our spending. A budget will give direction to our spending.

2. *A budget is a tool for measuring.* When we budget we can monitor how we are doing. We will be able to see our debt position improve. It becomes possible to know when we are beginning to reverse our spending patterns.

3. *A budget is a tool for control.* Once we understand how to make and maintain a budget correctly, we will be able to keep spending under control. At this point it is very important to know that making and maintaining a budget is not a difficult procedure, as we shall see in the following chapters.

The economic climate keeps changing. It is extremely important that our spending be guided, measured, and controlled. A budget can be used to get us out of general debt from all kinds of loans and credit card buying. A budget will also keep us out of this type of debt. Most of us will probably be making mortgage payments on our houses most of our lives. But we don't have to be in debt for all those other things.

From an airline magazine I clipped an article by Carol Stocker in which she said, ''Each of us is exposed to an average of 300 ads a day, according to the advertising agency Batten, Barton, Durstine, and Osborn. With competition for our attention so fierce, there's little wonder that the most memorable advertisements combine elements of creative genius and psychological warfare. One could argue that advertising has become our number one art form, combining much of the best photography, camera work, writing, and acting being done in America today.''

Simply restated, the most creative minds in the nation,

using the best equipment, the finest talent, and nearly an unlimited budget impact our minds and emotions 300 times a day to get us to buy things we may not need and may not even want. We need guidance, measurement, and control in our spending. I must add that Mary and I had no more money, or basic intelligence, or time, or resources than any other couple. What we were doing with our money and budget was what any couple can do. It is possible for us to budget our way to freedom.

We need guidance, measurement, and control. We need a budget.

10 / How to Make a Budget

This is not a course in accounting but rather a lesson in accountability. One does not have to be an accountant or to have had even high school bookkeeping in order to follow this program. In fact, you would be surprised to know how many accountants and bookkeepers don't even have a personal and family budget. This system is simple and straightforward, something that can be understood and used.

FIVE STEPS TO MAKING A BUDGET

1. Take out a piece of paper and write down why you have not been on a budget. Did you feel it was too complicated? Too much work? Perhaps you simply did not know how to budget. You will know by the end of this chapter. If you can be honest enough, maybe your ego has not allowed you to admit that you need to keep track of what is going on financially. Whatever the reason is, write it down.

2. Next, list the results of your not being on a budget. Are you in debt? Heavily? You don't seem to have money to go places and do things? Is it necessary for you to say over and over to your children, "We can't afford that"? Do you and your spouse fight and argue about money? Mary and I did.

Does the pressure build around your house when it comes time to pay the bills each month? Are you getting calls and notes about past due accounts? Go ahead. Be honest. Put it down on paper: what are the results of your not being on a budget?

3. You must make a commitment to budgeting. There must be that moment for you, if you are single, or both of you, if you are married, to decide you will budget. You are not going to *try* to budget but you *will* budget.

I usually suggest something that may sound silly, but I have learned that it works. Write out a statement of commitment and then sign it. If you are married, both of you must sign it because you will not be totally successful unless you both agree to it. Partially successful, yes. You can do something by yourself, but if you are married then you both need to make a commitment, something like this:

MY / OUR BUDGET COMMITMENT

I / We, the undersigned, choose to commit my / our energy to eighteen months of intensive budgeting discipline and procedures, beginning _____.

                                 month   day   year

Signature _____

Date _____

Signature _____

Date _____

There is a reason why you should sign a commitment. What is almost the first thing a child learns in kindergarten? Answer: To write his or her name. From that moment until the person dies, signing his name commits him. Every paper handed in during school years must have a name on it. When one goes for a driver's license, he signs his name. A car is purchased and the buyer signs his name. Purchase agreements and credit buying require signatures. Signing one's name commits the signer. So a budget commitment should have signatures as well.

Should you or your spouse begin to ignore the procedures of good budgeting you should go back to the statement and remind yourselves or each other what you should be doing.

4. When you are ready to begin entering things into the budget, start first with those items you know are fixed costs. These will be such things as car payments, house payments, insurance premiums, or other contract payments.

5. Finally go back over the budget and put in the items that may vary as to the amount spent per month, such as clothing, food, gasoline, and other nonfixed expenses.

EXAMINE THE BUDGET SHEETS

If you are using copies of the Personal Budget Sheets prepared by Planned Living, spread them out before you. If these sheets are not available refer to Figures A1 and A2 shown on the following pages.

You will notice that your budget can start any month. You don't have to wait until next January. At the top of the sheets you simply write in the month and the year.

To the left of the page is a column titled *Reserve Carried Forward.* This is to be explained later, so disregard that column for the moment.

The widest column on the page is the second column from the left titled *Category and Account.* You will notice there are fourteen categories listed: *Giving, Savings, Investments, Home, Living Expenses, Transportation, Credit Cards* (to be used to get you off of them), *Personal, Medical & Dental, Education, Entertainment, Gifts, Travel,* and *Insurance.*

Next you will notice the third column which is called *Monthly Budget Amount.* It is here that you will write in how much money you are going to budget per month for each of the categories and accounts listed.

Next come the columns numbered 1 through 31. These are for the days of the month and it is here that you will write down daily expenditures. Don't get nervous. In the next chapter, on how to stay on a budget, you are going to see how really easy this is to do.

The next column following the numbered 1 through 31 column is the *Monthly Category Totals*. This is where, at the end of the month, you will take out your calculator and add up the money spent on days 1 through 31 in each category and account during the month. For example, let's say you spent on dry cleaning $5.50 on March 9, $3.75 on March 17, and $9.50 on March 26. When you total up your expenditures for the month you would have spent $18.75 for dry cleaning. That amount would then be placed in the column titled *Monthly Category Totals* (see Figure B).

The next to the last column on the right is to tell you whether you spent more or less money than budgeted for each item. This column is titled *This Month's Category Reserves* and the numbers written in this column will be preceded by either a plus (+) or minus (–) sign. The plus sign means you have spent during the month less than you budgeted, (the figure written in the *Monthly Budget Amount* column), so you have more available for that account next month. If you are budgeting the correct amount, in several months the numbers will more or less level out. If each month you are constantly running a minus number and you are being as economical as reasonably possible, it shows you are not allowing enough in the budget each month to cover this ongoing expense. But do not attempt to correct it until it is time to revise the entire budget, as we will discuss later.

Let's go back to the example of the dry cleaning. You have spent a total of $18.75 for the month. Had you budgeted $25 (the amount listed in the *Monthly Budget Amount* column) and had thus spent only $18.75 of it, you would have in the column titled *This Month's Category Reserves* +6.25. You would find this by the following accounting:

Month's Budget Amount	$25.00
Monthly Category Totals	18.75
This Month's Category Reserves	+6.25

This means that next month you will have an additional $6.25 to be added to your dry cleaning budget and used if

MONTHLY BUDGET: EXPENSE RECORD _____ 19____

Reserve Carried Forward	Category and Account	Monthly Budget Amount	1	2	3	4	5	6	7	8
	1. GIVING: Church									
	Charities									
	Other									
	2. SAVINGS: Bank									
	Bonds									
	Credit Unions									
	Other									
	3. INVESTMENTS: Stocks									
	Bonds									
	Other									
	4. HOME: Mortgage/Rent									
	Taxes									
	Heat									
	Light									
	Water & Sewer									
	Garbage									
	Telephone									
	Maintenance									
	Improvements									
	Furniture									
	Appliances									
	Other									
	5. LIVING EXPENSES: Food									
	Clothing									
	Dry Cleaning									
	Other									
	6. TRANSPORTATION: Car Payment									
	Car Insurance									
	Licenses									
	Car Maintenance									
	Fares/Tolls/Parking									
	Gasoline & Oil									
	Other									
	7. CREDIT CARDS:									

Figure A-1

16 17 18 19 20 21 22 23 24 25 26 27 28 29 30 31	Monthly Category Totals	This Month's Category Reserves	Category Balances Owed

Reserve Carried Forward	Category and Account	Monthly Budget Amount	1	2	3	4	5	6	7	8
	8. PERSONAL: Beauty / Barber Shops									
	N.P. Drugs & Sundries									
	Wife's Allowance									
	Husband's Allowance									
	Children's Allowances									
	Other									
	9. MEDICAL & DENTAL: Medical									
	Dental									
	P. Drugs									
	Transportation									
	10. EDUCATION: Tuition & Fees									
	Books & Supplies									
	Transportation									
	Periodicals & Magazines									
	Other									
	11. ENTERTAINMENT: Sports Events									
	Concerts									
	Movies									
	Eating Out									
	Other Recreation									
	Other									
	12. GIFTS: Birthdays									
	Christmas									
	Other Special Occasions									
	Other									
	13. TRAVEL: Vacation									
	Other									
	14. INSURANCE: Home									
	Possessions									
	Life									
	Health									
	Other									
	TOTAL MONTHLY EXPENSES:									

Figure A-2

5	16	17	18	19	20	21	22	23	24	25	26	27	28	29	30	31	Monthly Category Totals	This Month's Category Reserves	Category Balances Owed

BUDGET: EXPENSE RECORD _March_ 19 _83_

MONTH   YEAR

Category and Account	Monthly Budget Amount	1 2	3 9 10 15 16 17 18 5 26 27	Monthly Category Totals
GIVING: Church				
Charities				
Other				
SAVINGS: Bank				
Bonds				
Credit Unions				
Other				
INVESTMENTS: Stocks				
Bonds				
Other				
HOME: Mortgage / Rent				
Taxes				
Heat				
Light				
Water & Sewer				
Garbage				
Telephone				
Maintenance				
Improvements				
Furniture				
Appliances				
Other				
LIVING EXPENSES: Food				
Clothing				
Dry Cleaning	25.00		5.50 3.75 9.50	18.75
Other				
TRANSPORTATION: Car Payment				
Car Insurance				
Licenses				
Car Maintenance				
Fares / Tolls / Parking				
Gasoline & Oil				
Other				
CREDIT CARDS:				

Figure B   ©

ENSE RECORD *March* 19 83

MONTH   YEAR

	Monthly Budget Amount	1	8	9	10	11	17	18	26	27	1	Monthly Category Totals	This Month's Category Reserves	Cate Bala Owe
ions														
ks														
ds														
er														
Rent														
ewer														
ce														
ents														
s														
Food														
Clothing														
Dry Cleaning	15.00			5.50			3.75		9.50			18.75	-3.75	
Other														
Car Payment														
Car Insurance														
Licenses														
Car Maintenance														
Fares / Tolls / Parking														
Gasoline & Oil														
Other														

Figure C

you choose to do so. This amount will be carried over to the next month's sheet and entered in the first column, *Reserve Carried Forward.*

The opposite would also be true. Let's say you have spent the same $18.75 on dry cleaning but you had budgeted only $15.00. Now what? You total expenditures the same as before and place the $18.75 figure in the column marked *Monthly Category Totals.* Now you can tell from the difference between your budgeted amount and your expenditures that you have spent $3.75 more than you budgeted, so you will put in the column marked *This Month's Category Reserves* −3.75 (see Figure C). This means you have spent more than you budgeted and next month you will have $3.75 less to spend for dry cleaning if you stay within the budget. Here is how you come to this amount:

$$\begin{array}{ll}\text{Monthly Category Budget} & \$15.00 \\ \text{Monthly Category Totals} & \underline{18.75} \\ \text{This Month's Category Reserves} & -3.75 \end{array}$$

The final column on the far right of the page is titled *Category Balances Owed.* This is the place where Mary and I keep track of our declining balances. It becomes a motivational column. It is fun and encouraging to watch the balance on our car go down. Especially exciting is to see the balance on our credit cards going down as we learn how to get out of credit card debt. I have called credit card debt *The Plastic Prison.*

EXAMINE THE BUDGET
CATEGORY BY CATEGORY

As you go down through the budget, notice some guidelines as to how to put a budget together. Before you begin writing your own estimates you should finish reading the entire third section on budgeting in order to get the overall picture before the budget is started.

1. *Giving.* I believe we ought to start our Christian giving at 10 percent of gross salary. Some people want to give on the net salary but I ask, "Do you want God to bless you on your gross or your net?" I want a blessing on the gross.

Something should be put aside for other charities. The Girl Scouts are going to come around as will the mother's and grandmother's march, the local Christian school, and your favorite political party

2. *Savings.* Good fiscal planning demands that you save 10 percent. We might say our tenth to God has to do with eternal affairs and the other tenth to saving has to do with temporal affairs. You should keep in the bank in a liquid account at least three times your net monthly salary and better yet six times the amount you take home. In case of illness or accident you can then continue to take care of yourself and your family until the temporary crisis is over

3. *Investments.* This book is not to teach you how to make money or where to invest it. It is enough to say here that investment should be a carefully planned program that fits in with your other monetary plans.

4. *Home.* Start by entering the amount of your house payment or rent. If your house payment includes taxes and insurance then leave those items blank when you come to them.

The next four items, heat, light, water and sewer, and garbage will probably vary as to the area of the country where you live and the season of the year. You do not pay the same amount for heat in Seattle that you pay in Minnesota Nor do you pay the same amount for heat in July as you do in January unless you are on some company budget payment plan. With items like these you will want to average them out so you are setting aside a fixed amount of money per month. Thus in some months you will be banking money so that in other months you will have it to pay the bigger bills when they come.

GO THROUGH PAST RECORDS

To come up with these averages you should take your heating bills for last year, add them up, put in any inflationary factor or rate increase of which you are aware, and divide that amount by twelve to find the monthly amount needed. Put that final monthly figure in the *Monthly Budget Amount* column. When the monthly bill is less than the budget amount you will be building up a reserve in that account. When the bill is more than the monthly budget amount you will be drawing on the reserve you have built up earlier. This safety cushion is part of what we mean by removing the surprises from your financial planning.

KEEP TRACK FOR A MONTH

If you have no idea what you spend in some of the categories, you may want to keep track of what you spend for a month. Then you should study the figure and determine whether or not that was an average month and make adjustments. Use this information as a guide for budgeting. Should it be that you have never kept track of expenditures before, you may be in for a real surprise.

At a Planning Living Seminar a man said, "My wife and I kept track of everything we spent for one month, even what we put on our credit cards. When we added it all up we had spent so much more than we made, it scared us so bad we never did it again." How do you argue with that kind of logic?

However you decide to do it, you will need to average out your expenditures in order to know how much of your monthly budget should go toward that item, since your monthly income is a fixed amount.

Next is the *telephone*. It is jokingly said that one can figure his phone bill by how far away his in-laws are from him. I can add from experience it also makes a difference how far away the children and grandchildren live. Average the year's total and then add a little for those times of emergency with health and accident.

Home maintenance is an item often overlooked. The least you can plan for in home maintenance is 1 percent of the appraised value of the house. This amount needs to be set aside annually. So if your house is valued at $60,000 you need to put at least $600 aside each year to maintain it. That amounts to $50 a month. If you were to start this and continue it, you would not need a second mortgage for a new roof. Your department store would not see you showing up with your credit card to buy house paint. You would not find a knot in the pit of your stomach when you have to call an electrician or a plumber.

For the next three items, *improvements, furniture,* and *appliances,* you need to set aside annually another 1 percent of the appraised value of your home. Again if your home has a $60,000 value, you should put aside an additional $600, or $50 per month. Do this faithfully and you will be able to get your new drapes and the new washer or dryer when the old one dies.

5. *Living Expenses.* Be realistic when you come to these items of food and clothing. Occasionally people feel they spend hardly anything on clothes. But stop for a moment and think. For instance, it is August and you are buying school clothes for a fourteen-year-old boy. He needs three pairs of jeans, about five shirts, socks, and tee shirts, plus a pair of school shoes; then a pair of "name brand" tennis shoes, gym shoes for school, a winter coat, and, if he plays soccer or football, shoes for the sport. You have just spent about $400 and he has nothing to wear to church or for a special occasion. Walk a family of four through that kind of process and you will have them spending about $150 per month on clothes. People are living like this today, so when you begin to budget for food and clothing, be realistic. You don't gain anything by playing games of wishful thinking with yourself about how much money you spend.

6. *Transportation*. Next to the home the biggest purchase most Americans will ever make is the automobile. Actually it may be one of our worst purchases. Cars are very expensive, a luxury that our system or life-style has turned into a necessity.

One of the major car rental agencies says that to own and operate a car costs us forty-three cents per mile. That figure may be a little high in some cases. But if every time we drove one mile we would put forty-three cents in savings we could take care of our car and replace it. Think through what your car or cars are really costing you and fill in the budgeting section under transportation. This figure is arrived at by totaling the cost of the car, all gasoline and oil, maintenance, insurance, taxes, tires, licensing and city stickers you expect to pay for during the life of that car. Then subtract the selling price or trade-in value and divide the remainder by the number of miles you intend to drive the car to get the cost per mile rate.

One of the purposes of budgeting is to rid yourself of surprises. Be sure you budget enough for transportation. It will lead you to a sense of freedom.

7. *Credit Cards*. In 1981 Jay Easton, expert on consumer credit, reported the following in *U. S. News and World Report*: "The number of single people in trouble is growing, particularly the single women segment. The typical income is in the $12,000 to $16,000 range, and the typical debt burden—excluding the home mortgage—is $8,200, compared to $5,700 for most families."

I am not an economist, but I do understand one thing— you cannot spend more money than you make, and survive. Yet this is exactly what is happening all over our nation as people use their credit cards freely.

Think of it—the average family at $5,700 in debt and the average single person at $8,200. Don't even begin to compute the interest these people are paying with some of the credit card rates now at over 20 percent. It is frightening.

You must get off those charge cards—now. In a later

chapter we will discuss what to do with credit cards, but for now, determine to set money aside for expenditures so you will not need to use the cards. This is called budgeting, a written statement of estimated income and expenses.

On the budgeting sheets there is a place for credit cards, not to encourage their use but rather to encourage their retirement. Write in the name of the company under the words credit cards and for the *Monthly Budget Amount* write in the minimum payment required or more, if you think you can pay more. Then in the last column on the far right, called *Category Balance Owed,* write in the amount you still owe on the card. As you do this each month the balance owed will be reduced. It becomes a game, actually enjoyable to see that amount being reduced and finally wiped out. When that happens it will be just like giving yourself a raise of however much you have been paying each month.

If you don't use the card for a while and start paying off the balance you will probably get some type of letter or mailer from the company whose card you are paying off asking you to come in and use the card. They want to keep you on the hook.

I have seen budgets where the minimum payments on their credit cards amounted to $350 to $500 or more. Cure this problem in your home. Follow through on the commitment you have signed to budget.

8. *Personal.* Here is where we record such expenses as the barber and beauty shop, cosmetics, all the things we squirt, rub on, paint on, wipe off, and spray. Think carefully about what is spent each year in this area. The average family of four usually spends more than $50 per month in this category. Be realistic and honest. You will be surprised what you are paying for these items.

Next count up how much is spent for nonprescription drugs and sundries such as toothpaste, aspirin, cold remedies, vitamins, and food supplements.

Are you ready for this?—the *wife's allowance.* I have deep feelings about this. I contend that every woman needs some money that is entirely her own. She does not need to buy food or pantyhose or things for the kids out of this amount. This allowance is hers to do with as she wants. Should she be a part of a local Bible study or women's club she can stop with the girls on the way home and have lunch. Or she can use this for her handicrafts or whatever she likes.

There are two reasons I take the time to mention this. First, the women are going to do these things anyway, and rightly so. Second, if the money is not designated as theirs they feel as if they are taking it from the food budget or somewhere else in the family's financial plan. Then they feel guilty when they should be having a good time.

How much should be allowed for this category? I don't know. Does $30 sound like too much? Is your wife worth a dollar a day all her own? Frankly, it is more than most of them get.

When you begin to figure the husband's allowance, remember he does not have the opportunity to go to the refrigerator and open the door anytime he wants while he is at work. There are some things that make the situation for him a little different.

Sorry, I can't relate to *children's allowances*. We always paid our boys a salary. But that is a subject for the next book or seminar on how to teach your children to be goal setters. People tell me they give their children $5 a week. It doesn't seem like much because you can't do much with $5, but for two children that would amount to $40 per month. Interesting, isn't it, how quickly things add up.

9. *Medical and Dental*. These items are self-explanatory. Under that heading is an item for transportation. If you are having excessive medical problems you may want to keep track of this for the purpose of your income taxes.

10. *Entertainment*. Most of us do not hold season passes to professional sporting events but we do spend dollars and lots of them on these occasions. For instance, my boys are wrestlers. There were two matches a week for ten weeks. Mary and I tried to make each match. If we did, it would

have cost us $2 each or $4 per match, $8 per week, thus $80 for ten weeks. Then the three tournaments were $3 for the morning and afternoon sessions and an additional $2 for the evening or $5 per person for the day. So if we both went it cost $10 per day and if the tournament was two days it would be $20. In a season it was easy for us to spend up to $150 on entrance fees—more than $12 per month. Frankly, we spent it and saw nothing more than our boys sweat and strain for six minutes if the match went the full distance.

Concerts are big these days, both inside and outside the church community. Budget for them if you are going to spend the money.

For a movie you will spend about $4 per ticket, plus $1 for twenty cents' worth of popcorn and seventy-five cents for ten cents' worth of drink. If a family of four takes in a movie, providing they can find one worth attending, they will leave $20 in the theater.

You don't go to the movies, you say? Well, what about cable TV and Home Box Office? Budget your entertainment, whatever it is.

Eating out is something you should have in your budget. At least once per month you and your spouse should go on a date. Plan a dinner without the children. At a moderately priced restaurant including tip it will cost you about $25 for the evening—more if you need a baby-sitter. By moderately priced, I mean somewhere with the lights so low you can hardly read the menu or tell what you are eating.

Other recreation? What about skiing, tennis, jogging, back-packing, camping, sailing, water skiing, surfing, fishing, bowling, even golfing? Be honest, you are doing them, so budget for them. They cost you dollars.

12. *Gifts.* Oh, Lanson, don't be so foolish! I'm not being foolish. We spend hard-earned dollars on birthdays, anniversaries, Christmas, weddings, baby showers, Mother's Day, Mother-in-law's Day, Valentine's Day, and others. If you are spending money on them, put them in the budget.

13. *Vacation.* A family of four will be hard pressed to

travel to a vacation spot such as Disneyland, the San Juans, the Grand Canyon, and do it on less than $100 per day, so a nine-day vacation comes to $75 per month.

14. Finally, there is the space for *Insurance*. You are paying these premiums, so budget for them. Remember that some house payments, at the bank's insistence, include the taxes and insurance. It doesn't matter where that kind of insurance is recorded, either under *Home Mortgage/Rent* or under *Insurance,* so long as it is recorded only once in one place or the other.

Don't be in a hurry to put your budget figures down. You are going to be living with this for at least six months so take your time and think through all your expenses.

THE EIGHTEEN-MONTH COMMITMENT

You were asked to sign a commitment for eighteen months so that if you budget for that long you will not want to get off it. When you start budgeting use the same *Monthly Budget Amount* for each category and account for six months. The reason for this is that it will usually take you about six months really to learn and understand your spending patterns. After six months you should go ahead and revise your budget if it seems wise and use the new *Monthly Budget Amounts* assigned to categories for the next six months. This will bring you to the end of the first year.

Launch right into a second year, revising the figures for the coming year. By the end of eighteen months you will be so sold on budgeting that you will not want to leave it and you will wonder how you ever got along before you had it.

It takes about six months to begin to see what is really happening in your spending and to go through the pain of disciplining yourself to follow the budget procedures. The second six months you will begin to see the effect it is having on your life and the third six months you will be sold on it and will want to continue.

I taught the budgeting plan to a group of pastors. One of

them asked me to come to his church for a seminar. At the seminar he told his people he had been on a budget for four months. He went on to relate how in those four months he had been able to buy his children clothes on a sale because he had the cash and that he and his wife had been out to dinner three times. They had been on more husband and wife dates than in the two previous years. It pays to budget.

Note: Budget sheets as used in this book are available from Planned Living Seminars, 13740 Riviera Place, N.E., Seattle, WA 98125.

11 / Where Do I Keep All the Money?

Does this chapter title seem strange to you? It shouldn't, because from now on you are going to have money to keep. But first, let's look at some problem areas and considerations.

YOUR BUDGET MUST BALANCE

When you begin to put down the *Monthly Budget Amount* in each category, don't bother to keep a running total of how much you are allotting. Put down what you think you need to spend in each category. Then when you are all done, add it up and if you are normal you will find that you think you need to spend more than you are making.

Now go back over the budget and see what things you can combine. For example, some of the clothing allowance can be handled through your Christmas giving. Realize you have a gas and food allowance for the month of your vacation and those things will help you to reduce your monthly vacation allotment.

You must keep cutting back until your expenditures do not exceed your income. Perhaps your debt problem is such that you are not able to put away the full amounts in home maintenance, furniture, appliances, and clothes. I encourage you to put something in each account every month so you get in the habit and so that you will have at least something available to help you when the expenditure is needed. When you get your credit cards paid off, it will be like getting a raise and then you can put more away in some of the accounts that are a little slim.

It might be at the start that you can't save the full 10 percent but save something—even if it is only 1 percent. Get in the habit of adding something to every account. Whatever you do, don't short God. You honor him and he will honor you.

It is easier to make the decisions now that will keep you living within your income than it is to figure out how to get out of debt later.

WHAT IF MY INCOME CHANGES?

There are those salespeople who, because of a commission structure, find that their income varies. Also, certain types of trade workers are quite seasonal in their income.

My suggestion is that you take the last year or maybe the last two years of income and average it over twenty-four months. If you budget within that amount then you must put aside the money from the best months to take care of the lean months. If you are in this type of circumstance you are better off to be very conservative in estimating your income. It will keep you out of difficulty. I have found that for one reason or another my income is almost always less than my projections. Let's face it—it is harder to make it than it is to spend it.

MOVING FROM MONTH TO MONTH

Let's say you have just finished a month of budgeting. Now what do you do? You first total up what you have spent in each category. Next you check the amount spent against the amount budgeted. Don't forget, if you spent less than you budgeted it means you will have a plus (+) figure, the difference between what was budgeted and what was spent. This means you have that much more to spend next month. But if you have spent more than was budgeted, then you will have a minus (–) figure, the difference between what was spent and what was budgeted. This minus figure goes into the column *This Month's Category Reserves*.

Once you have done this for all the categories and accounts then take out new budget sheets and proceed in the following manner:

1. Put the new month and year at the top of the budget sheets.

2. Enter the same *Monthly Budget Amount* as you had last month unless you are at the end of a six-month period and feel it is necessary to revise the budget.

3. Now in the first column on the left, which has been totally ignored until now, you enter the amount from last month's column titled *This Month's Category Reserves*. In other words in the new month you will be putting in the carry over of surplus (+) or deficit (–) as a result of the last month's spending.

WHAT DOES THIS TELL ME?

To see what this is saying to you, go back to our example of the dry cleaning mentioned in Chapter 10. You will recall you spent $5.50 on the 9th, $3.75 on the 17th and $9.50 on the 26th for a total of $18.75. In our illustration of having budgeted $25 we then had +6.25 in the category *This Month's Reserve Balance*. This amount will be transferred to the *Reserve Carried Forward* for the next month. You will have the same amount budgeted in the new month, $25. This means that you have, reading from the left of your budget sheets, +$6.25 reserve and $25 budgeted for a total to spend on dry cleaning in that month of $31.25.

Again the opposite is also true. Back to our example, if you had spent the same $18.75 but had budgeted only $15 then you would have in *This Month's Category Reserve* – $3.75. When you carry over this amount to the next month's *Reserve Carried Forward* you would have – $3.75 and $15 which means you would have only $11.25 to spend on dry cleaning that month. Now you must alter your expenditures in that category until you make up this amount. If the difference is so great it can't all be made up in one month, then you must continue cutting back in subsequent months until you bring the account back into line with the *Monthly Budget Amount.*

This is one of the reasons I call the seminar I teach on this subject Planned Living. When the budget is out of line, call a family conference and see what you all can do together to bring it back into line. Plan your living. It is time you choose to be in control of your circumstances. Don't allow your creditors and circumstances to control you.

WHAT YOU ARE REALLY DOING

You probably see by now that through budgeting you are seeking to keep each account in balance each month. Keep it as simple as possible

WHAT IF I HAVE BIG PLUSES AND BIG MINUSES?

Often I'm asked what to do when someone has budgeted, for example, too much in clothing and not enough in eating out. Can they transfer from one account to another? Well, you can do anything you want—it is your budget. But, once you start that, you have gone from accountability back to accounting and chances are almost certain that you won't stay on the budget if you do. It will become too much of a hassle. Soon you will be so mixed up you will get discouraged and quit.

Make up your mind to keep each account in balance each month. If it isn't and you are short, then simply alter your living until you get it back in balance.

BUT WHAT ABOUT ALL THAT MONEY?

Perhaps you have surmised that funds will begin to build up in these accounts. Decide now to bank where you get interest on your checking account. Usually you need to keep a certain balance of $300 or so to collect the interest. Let that become your bottom figure rather than zero. At the end of the month transfer the reserves to a savings account where it will draw more interest and as soon as they build up to where you have enough to put into some higher interest-paying account put it there. It becomes a joy to watch your money earn interest instead of your having to pay interest to someone. Remember the motto: "Successful people spend their time doing the things unsuccessful people don't want to do." You *can* budget! Just follow directions.

12 / How to Stay on the Budget

At one time or another most of us have tried to maintain a budget of some kind. Perhaps we have gone to the office supply store and purchased some budget sheets or maybe even sought to make our own. Then somewhere along the line we learned it was one thing to make a budget and another thing to stay on it.

FOUR SIMPLE STEPS FOR STAYING ON A BUDGET

1. You must write down *all* expenses. You and your spouse or you alone if you are single need to buy a pocket-sized notebook to carry. Personally I use a system that allows me to put all my appointments, things to be done, diary of what I do, and a place for expenses all in one coat-sized pocket wallet. You do not need such an elaborate system. One of those small 3 x 5 spiral memo books will do. You can buy them at any stationery counter and most food stores. They will fit in a man's shirt pocket or a lady's purse.

It is not a difficult task to keep track of expenditures. When you reach for your money you must also reach for your notebook. For example, suppose you have eaten lunch at a restaurant. When you go to pay the bill you hand the cashier the money and the billing. As the cashier is ringing up the sale and making change you take out your book and write down the expenditure and what it was for. It will not take you any longer than it does for the cashier to make the change.

At this point you are probably wondering what I mean by *all* expenditures. I mean *all* expenditures. I can take you back through my book and show you where I have put ten cents in a parking meter or spent twenty-five cents on a newspaper or a phone call. Get in this habit and you will find your spending guided, measured, and controlled. Remember the purpose of a budget.

You might think this is stupid but let me give you the motto again: "Successful people will do the things that unsuccessful people don't want to do." People who are budgeting successfully are the ones who are writing down all expenses.

I can't begin to tell you how many letters I have received from seminar attendees who were stunned when they began to write down *all* expenditures to see what they had been spending and where.

2. You must transfer these expenditures to the budget book. Let me show you how easy this is to do. Place your budget book on your dresser in the bedroom. "Why there?" you might ask. Because most people go through a certain routine when they get ready for bed.

Make it a part of your nightly routine to transfer the figures from the book you carry to the budget book. If you have made five expenditures in a day, chances are for most of us it will be a big day. How long will it take you to write those figures in the budget book? Sixty seconds or even ninety seconds—no more. Is it worth an investment of one minute a night to get out of debt and stay out of debt?

Remember, the key is to do it daily. If you wait until the end of the week and try to resurrect all the expenditures you will hate yourself, hate budgeting, and will not stay on it. Again I say, "Successful people do the things unsuccessful people don't want to do."

3. Monitor the progress weekly. This is also a simple thing to do. You don't need to check every amount, but only those things that vary and things you intend to use in the coming week. How much money do you have left to spend? You noticed a sale coming next weekend on children's clothes. Where are you in the clothing budget?

Saturday night seems to be a good time for this. I have watched Mary do it while she sits under the hair dryer. Also this is a good time to remind yourself to write a God-honoring check that well represents your devotion to him.

This next step will get you out of debt and keep you out of debt.

4. Before you make an expenditure, go to the budget book and see if you have the money in reserve. If you don't have it in reserve, then don't spend it.

But what if it is a bargain? No bargain is a bargain if you don't have the money in reserve. Also there is always another bargain coming along. They are like busses. Wait a little while and another one will come.

Once you have begun the budgeting process, you no longer ask the question, "Do I have money in the checkbook?" You will have money in the checkbook. In fact, as those accounts build up you will have lots of money in the checkbook and the bank. That is no longer a valid question. The proper question is, "Do I have the money in reserve in the budget?"

This final step is what will turn your financial picture around or make it even better than it is now.

Here is what one young newspaper editor wrote:

"My checkbook and money management was pitiful before I attended a Planned Living Seminar. Although I originally planned to cover Mr. Ross's visit as a possible news story, it became quite clear to me that I should put down my professional note pad and begin jotting down items on a personal level. After living from paycheck to paycheck regardless of how much I made, I was genuinely amazed at how much money I was spending without even thinking about it. By placing myself on a personal budget, I find I think much more before I buy and I buy much less. Unexpected emergencies like car breakdowns no longer leave me floundering from bank to bank for a loan—I now have money set aside for just such occurrences.''

One more time—you can do it. ''Successful people spend their time doing the things unsuccessful people don't want to do.''

13 / The Plastic Prison

There are debt counselors who tell us to go home and cut up our credit cards. I am not going to tell you to do that. But if you are out of control, or have a tendency to get out of control with credit buying, then take your cards, put a rubber band around them, and put them in a drawer under your winter underwear that you use only once a year.

If you can't cash a check without some identification, then you will have to carry a couple, but carry those ones least likely to get you in trouble, such as gasoline credit cards. Better yet, plan ahead and you won't need to carry any.

The only thing the credit card means is that some bank or establishment has approved you to have a certain amount of money advanced to you. It is the same as a loan. Think of it in this way. If I said to you, "Go down to the bank and borrow some money so you can take me to dinner," you would probably reply you would never consider a loan for such a thing. But when you put down your charge card for dinner you have just borrowed that amount of money. The rules are that if you pay back the bills when they come due, then they are a marvelous convenience, so we are told. But if you don't pay them back in full when you are billed, then you pay interest on them, and today some of those interest charges exceed 20 percent.

EMERGENCIES

There are cases of genuine emergency when your charge card might have to be used. Should you live in California and your mother in Illinois becomes terminally ill, you will want to go and be with her. If you don't have the money, you may need to use your charge card. That would be a true emergency. However, wanting a new lens for your camera is not an emergency. Neither is a new turntable for your stereo or a night out for the family. Do you have the money in the budget reserve? That is the question for those items.

Someone has well said, "Never use your credit card for items that depreciate, luxury items, nor for anything that can be eaten, or needs paint."

If you ever do need to use them and it is really an emergency, then do everything you can to pay them off as soon as possible. The interest on these cards is eating up the future of many people today.

Set your will to get out and stay out of the Plastic Prison. In the old days a fool and his money were soon parted. Now it is happening to more and more people, and it shouldn't be so.

SCRIPTURE REFERENCES TO BUDGETING

"Honor the Lord by giving him the first part of all your income, and he will fill your barns with wheat and barley and overflow your wine vats with the finest wines" (Proverbs 3:9, 10).

"The good man's earnings advance the cause of righteousness. The evil man squanders his on sin" (Proverbs 10:16).

"Steady plodding brings prosperity; hasty speculation brings poverty" (Proverbs 21:5).

"The wise man saves for the future, but the foolish man spends whatever he gets" (Proverbs 21:20).

"Riches can disappear fast. And the king's crown doesn't

stay in his family forever—so watch your business interests closely. Know the state of your flocks and your herds, then there will be lamb's wool enough for clothing, and goat's milk enough for food for all your household after the hay is harvested, and the new crop appears, and the mountain grasses are gathered in'' (Proverbs 27:23-27).

FAMOUS QUOTATIONS ABOUT BUDGETING

"I've got all kinds of money but it is tied up in debts." —Anonymous

"God says: 'Take what you want and pay for it!'" —Spanish Proverb

"The reason most of us don't live within our income is because we don't consider that living."—Anonymous

"The best place to spend your vacation this summer is somewhere near your budget."—Anonymous

"We will never get anywhere with our finances until we pass a law saying that every time we appropriate something we got to pass another bill along with it stating where the money is coming from."—Will Rogers

"What seems so necessary today may not even be desirable tomorrow."—Anonymous

"One sees the strangest things sometimes. Like that fellow buying a money belt—and charging it."—Anonymous

"The founder and owner of a large department store was asked the secret of his success. 'Well, you know, I was just a poor farm boy—never did get much schoolin'. And when you don't know much you've got to use your brains.'"

PART FOUR
HOW TO MAKE
DECISIONS IN
A CRISIS HOUR

14 / Decision Makers Are People of Faith

Our lives are like a film clip. They are pieces of time clipped out of eternity in which we make decisions. All of our lives we will be making decisions—thousands of them, millions of them. They involve our eating, our working, our appearance, our families, our future, and our eternal destiny.

Most of the decisions are so small that we make them hardly thinking about them. Many actually become habit patterns. We encounter more important decisions such as vocation, education, marriage, investments, and many more.

Then on occasion there will appear in our lives a real crisis. It might come in the form of broken health, or severe financial setback. For others crisis takes the form of an overwhelming marriage problem.

I am convinced that it is the difficult things of life that build character and strength, not the easy things. James spoke to this issue: "Dear brothers, is your life full of difficulties and temptations? Then be happy, for when the way is rough, your patience has a chance to grow. So let it grow, and don't try to squirm out of your problems. For when your patience is finally in full bloom, then you will be ready for anything, strong in character, full and complete" (James 1:2-4).

It is a fact that great generals are made in war—not in peace.

DON'T PANIC; GET SYSTEMATIC!

Several times in my life I have been in what I feel were crisis situations. They were times when what I did with the problems confronting me would determine a great portion of my future and my family's future.

While pastoring in Vancouver, Washington, I had a problem with my health. I was thirty-one years of age. I awoke in the middle of the night feeling very strange and weak. As I attempted to get up I fell, feeling paralyzed on the left side of my body. Mary, of course, immediately called the ambulance. They came and took me to the emergency room of a nearby hospital.

At the time I did not know it, but when my wife arrived at the hospital they told her I could be having a stroke or a heart attack. My vital signs were such that they informed her there was a chance I might not make it through the night. They worked to control my system, left me in the hospital for a week, and gave me all the usual tests and more.

The doctor came in with a sort of good-news-bad-news story. The good news was that I was not going to die. The bad news was I had been living like a wild man and I had driven myself to complete emotional and physical exhaustion. With my poor self-image, I was serving out of guilt and self-condemnation. I was a mental, emotional, and physical wreck. It took me a year of struggle to come back from that experience. I had to make some decisions as to what I was going to do with my life.

THE PRESSURE OF BUSINESS

It is easy for any of us to become greedy. All we have to do is to allow our egos and natural desires to take over. During the days I was raising funds almost exclusively I had five accounts with which I was working. Things were going well and I was asked to do another account which, for a small organization such as mine, was a good-sized fund-raising effort. So I took the job and hired a man to oversee the work. I had worked with him before and he had done well in what I had asked of him. He was talented. However, I had made what I call the classical managerial mistake. This good man was now being asked to do something he could not do. Without going into all the details, it became obvious in about four months that he could not do the job. I had spent $43,000 of the up-front money and nothing had been raised. Material had been written, brochures, literature, and a good slide presentation started, but no money had been raised.

A crisis had arisen. It appeared to me that there were three choices. First, I could continue with the program as outlined and maybe make it, but the facts were saying it would fail. Second, I could stop what I was doing, give up the five accounts, go to this project and stay until it was finished. This was a great temptation because I did not want to face the facts and admit that I had made a mistake. The old ego was puffing up.

The time factors seemed to preclude bringing someone else into the picture. So, the third alternative was to terminate the project and pay back the $43,000 which had been spent.

What does a decision maker do when he makes a wrong decision? He makes another decision.

DECISIONS ARE BASED ON FAITH

Faith is the key word in the decision-making process. None of us knows when we make a decision exactly how things will turn out. When we enter into marriage it is or should be a life decision. One of us asks and the other accepts and promises are made in faith.

To quit one job and move on to another takes faith that things will turn out well. Buying a home, moving to a new area, purchasing an automobile—all of these things are decisions made in faith, trusting that time and sometimes even eternity will show that we have made the right decision.

THREE ANCHORS FOR YOUR FAITH

One of the fun things about cruising in our sailboat is to pull into a lonely anchorage just before dusk, set the anchor, eat a leisurely dinner and go to bed. I have seen the wind come up during the night to test the set of our anchor and the strength of the line holding us.

The decisions we make in life, particularly the ones made in crisis, will tell us some things about our faith.

1. We all need a bottom line in our lives, a foundation we can come back to when things are tough, maybe even going against us. The Lord is the bottom line for me. No matter what is going on in my life I have confidence that the Lord is not surprised by it and that he has not abandoned me. We have the promise of Jesus himself that he will never leave us nor forsake us.

Jesus and the disciples once crossed a lake in a boat. The Master was asleep when suddenly a storm arose. The disciples thought the boat was going to sink, so they called on Jesus to help them. The Scripture records how he stilled the storm and calmed the sea. The King James Bible expresses a beautiful thought: "And when he was entered into a ship, his disciples followed him" (Matthew 8:23). When your crisis is severe, remember that if you are a Christian the Lord got into the boat before you did, and no matter what the storm is he is able to take care of you.

Go back and read the section on self-image. God is not against you—he is for you. He wants you to be a "becomer." We are called to become something by his grace.

A study of the life of Jesus shows that he never called people because of what they were but for what he wanted them to become. Matthew, the tax collector, was hated by the people of his day, because he was a publican. He was a Jew who had sold himself out to the Roman government. As a publican he was responsible to Rome to collect taxes from other Jews. He was probably also lining his own pockets as most publicans were paid on something of a commission. The more the publicans could collect, honestly or dishonestly, the more they made. If a man's taxes were the equivalent of $500 and a publican thought he could get $600 out of him, he would charge him $600 and put the other $100 in his pocket. Jesus didn't call Matthew because he was a publican but because of what Jesus wanted Matthew to become.

Peter, a raw-boned, tough, impetuous fisherman, was not called by Jesus because he was a fisherman. Jesus called Peter because of what he wanted Peter to become—a servant. He wanted him to become an authority figure to carry the gospel message to the whole world.

This is what I mean by faith in God. I have faith that God has called me, not because of what I am but because of what he wants me to become. God has a task for my life. God has made me a man of destiny. There is a purpose that I am to live out in this world. There is reason for me to be on earth. I must exercise my gifts, talents, and abilities in order to fulfill that destiny.

The Lord is working in us and allowing things to come which will mold us and build us into an instrument of his glory.

2. Have faith in yourself. Ethel Waters once said, "God don't make no flops."

The Apostle James touched on one of the great truths of Christian living when he declared, "Faith without works is dead." You can never divorce yourself from responsibility in life. Don't even try it—it is a lost cause. "Casting all your care on him because he cares for you" does not imply that we are supposed to sit down and do nothing about our problems.

I can't accept that you and I can go out and mess up our lives, financially, morally, with our families, or any other way and then run to God and tell him we are sorry, and have lifted from us all responsibility for those things we have done. There are bills to be paid, apologies to be extended, and issues to be dealt with when we accept responsibility for our actions.

Nowhere in the Bible do I find God making himself responsible to subsidize bad management. We have no right to mess up our lives and then suddenly rush to God and expect him to put all the pieces back together.

"Don't you believe in miracles, Lanson?" Yes, I do. I have witnessed God's miracles. I believe that he can and does heal. He has arranged and rearranged circumstances in my life and the lives of those I know and love. There is no doubt in my mind that God is the God of miracles. Furthermore, he can give us a miracle any time he chooses to, but I don't think he ever owes us one.

There are many passages in the Word of God that tell us how we are to conduct ourselves and how we are to live and resist evil. The Lord has made us responsible for our actions and our choices. To make the right choices we must have faith in God and faith in ourselves.

3. It is perfectly proper to have faith in our abilities. Nothing is more nauseating than to find a person who knows he can do something and have to listen to him go through his false humility routine of "No, I just couldn't do that," when all the time he knows he can. This seems to be pride of the worst sort.

My wife is a good example of a person who knows what she can do. Mary is an excellent marimbist. I love to hear her play. When people come to our home and they see the marimba set up they often ask who plays. Mary will always say, "I do." More often than not the person asks if Mary will play something, to which she says, "Sure." And for a few minutes she dazzles them with what she can do. She knows she can play the instrument and she does not waste her time with false humility.

It is all right to know what you can do and have faith in yourself to be able to get a task done. This is not pride—it is confidence. I know God gave me these abilities, and I know he can take them away when he chooses. I try to give him the credit for being the giver of these gifts and abilities. But as long as I have them I believe he expects me to use them when they are needed.

I have learned from experience the things that I can do, and I am concentrating on what I know I can do. I no longer spend all my time struggling with things I can't do.

I am no good at fixing my car. I don't pretend anymore that I can. I'm not a plumber or an electrician. There are some things I like to do on my boat. I like to clean it, scrape and paint it, and do the simple maintenance items such as changing the oil. But I don't know electronics, engine work, and technical things beyond my limited skills. I hire people to do these. Through the years I have learned to concentrate on the things I can do.

You ask me, "How can I identify my gifts?"

Gift identification is a process. In this process we are allowed all the experiences we need. Some people might call these negative experiences when they don't work out. But when you find something you can't do, it doesn't mean you are a failure. It means you now know something you can't do, so you lay aside trying to do that sort of thing.

Thomas Edison finally found the elements for the filament of the incandescent light bulb. He had experimented for months. In fact, he put together over 8,000 experiments to find what he needed to make the light bulb shine as it does.

Someone asked him after he had made over 7,000 experiments if he wasn't discouraged with all his failures.

Edison replied, "Oh, my, no! I haven't had any failures. I now know 7,000 things that won't work."

It is the same story in learning what we can do. Rejoice every time you find something you can't do. Don't let it trouble you. Don't let it rob you of your energies. Determine to expend yourself in the areas that you find by experimentation you can do well.

Real dedication, I say again, is doing what you know you can do and choosing to do it for the honor and the praise of God.

15 / A Six-Step Decision-Making Process

The principles for getting me moving in a crisis have been put together as *acrostics,* an arrangement of words in which the first letter of each spells out a word.

I don't go through this process every time I make a decision. I use it when the mental tapes of my "brain computer" get stuck and no program is coming out. Then I turn to the following six things to get me moving again. The worst thing for me at such a time is to become mentally immobile. As long as I can get moving and keep moving the answers usually come.

1. The YES principle: The YES stands for Yield to Everything Sensible. By that I mean I don't spend my time fretting about what I can't do about a problem. I get busy on what I can do about it. There is always something that can be done. If nothing else, I get out a piece of paper and start outlining the problem and writing down any possible solutions, no matter how wild they seem at the time. Many times this exercise will start the creative juices flowing and lead me to a solution, or lead me to something or someone that will lead me to the solution.

Another way to state the YES principle is to use your common sense and do what you *can* do.

2. The PEN principle. After I have done everything I

know to do then I move on to the PEN principle, Pray
Earnestly Now. When I turn to God, I like to know that I
have done what I can about a problem. Then I feel more
relaxed about talking to him about his help.

God is very personal and I know from his Word that he is
interested in everything I am doing. None of what is happening to me is a surprise to him.

I have learned so much about my relationship with my
heavenly Father from being a father to my own two sons.
When a problem presents itself to them, maybe even one of
their own making, I watch them to see what they are going
to do about it. It has not been my habit to jump in immediately and solve it for them. There are certain things they
must learn. However, I always try to let them know I am
there to help them if they want it. They know I am interested
in them and that I am watching them. They also know that I
can usually help and will help them but they know that they
are responsible to do what they can. Both my boys and I
know that this is how they learn and mature. After they have
done what they can, I want them to come to me. Then we
are together in our plans and efforts in building their lives.

After I have done what I can, I pray because, after all,
God and I are together in the growing process of my life.

3. The SEE principle. At this point I use the SEE principle, Summon Every Experience. Once I have done all I can,
and have prayed, then I begin to ask, "Who do I know that
can help me with the next step? What experiences have I had
in the past that will help me now? Do I know anyone who
has gone through a similar thing and could I get some advice
or a new look at the problem by talking to him?"

I have often found that God has allowed me to go through
some past experience which is helpful now in solving my
present dilemma.

During a building project at a church where I was pastor,
we were under an extremely tight schedule. The staff member responsible for the project had failed to perform and now
the time was approaching when we had to complete the work.

First, I did everything I could to stimulate the man who

should have been responsible to get the job done. Seeing that was hopeless, I prayed and began making a list of everyone I had ever known who might have skill enough to complete the job. After calls to points near and far, the task was reassigned and finished on time.

This is what I mean by the SEE principle, Summon Every Experience you have had that will help you now.

4. Next, I use the GOD principle, which stands for God's Omnipotent Dealings. I know that God is powerful enough to help, no matter how great the problem. It is good to remind ourselves that God is often doing things for us we are not even aware he is accomplishing.

When Sarah was well past the time when she was able to have children, she laughed when the heavenly messengers told Abraham she would bear him a son. When questioned about her doubt, she heard this from the messenger: "Is anything too hard for God? Next year, just as I told you, I will certainly see to it that Sarah has a son" (Genesis 18:14).

At times our lives might seem unbearable. The pressures of business and family weigh us down until we wonder if it is worth it to keep going. Then in the midst of this a greater problem pops up. It is at such a time when we need to apply the GOD principle. He is all-powerful and adequate for any situation, so we must believe him and trust him.

No matter how bad it seems, God has not abandoned us.

5. The MAP principle. Next, you Make A Plan. A plan will begin to give you direction. To get out of a dilemma you need a direction. Remember, any plan is better than no plan. What you put down will probably not be the only possible plan or the best plan, but put it down, because it may lead you to the best plan.

Here is where the Bible becomes very important: "Any enterprise is built by wise planning, becomes strong through common sense, and profits wonderfully by keeping abreast of the facts" (Proverbs 24:3, 4).

So many people today have no plan. When they are faced with a difficult issue they do nothing because they plan nothing. To plan nothing is to plan to do nothing.

Get out a sheet of paper, put the pencil to it, and start writing about possibilities. You will be amazed how it will lead you to a plan.

6. The NAP principle. Sorry, I'm not talking about lying down and taking a nap. Rather, NAP means you Now Apply the Plan.

Motivators for years have taught, "Plan your work and work your plan." It is a valid principle and vital when you are in a crisis. Get in motion; nothing can be guided until it is in motion.

HOW THE PRINCIPLES WORK

Take the example of my $43,000 loss in business and examine how the principles were applied.

From a business standpoint, it was obvious that I needed to admit that I had made a mistake and get out of the contract by paying back the $43,000. There was one problem, or should I say forty-three thousand problems, and they were all dollars. The fact was that I didn't have that much money on hand.

1. The YES principle. First I Yielded to Everything Sensible. I did what I could do. Someone was going to have to finish the project for them and part of the work we had done could be used by those making the next effort. So the organization was willing to purchase those items from me at cost. Next there was equipment that could be sold, so I sold it. Also, I had some money on hand I could use to pay toward the remainder.

I was able to reduce the $43,000 down to $19,000, but I could not figure out how to pay the rest, and the people rightly wanted their money.

2. So I moved to the PEN principle. I began to Pray Earnestly Now, asking God to give me wisdom and direction. It is true God owns the cattle on a thousand hills, but as yet I have not met his auctioneer. What I'm saying is I didn't give $19 to some organization and go to the mail box and find a check for $19,000 from someone I had never seen

or heard from before or since. Other people tell me about such things but God has not led me that way.

3. Next I applied the SEE principle. I Summoned Every past Experience. I went to my management counselor for advice. My wife is a steady person. I respect her opinion. She was wise enough not to say, "I told you so."

Where had I gotten help before? What do I have I could use for collateral if I went to a bank? Every experience from my enterprising past was gone over and considered.

4. About here is where discouragement entered it. So I reminded myself of the GOD principle. "Lanson," I must have said to myself a hundred times and more, "even this is one of God's omnipotent dealings." I kept reminding myself that God had never failed me before and he was not going to this time.

My management counselor kept asking me when we would talk about how I felt. Finally I asked him why he wanted to know that and he said he had dealt with people who with this type of reversal had fallen into depression. Some, he said, had considered suicide. It is true that pressure can do strange things to the mind and the emotions.

It is good to know that we serve a God who is the same yesterday, today, and forever. He is not running out of power as times goes on.

5. It was then time to Make A Plan, the MAP principle. When this all happened, $19,000 was not available to me from any bank, so I sat down and made a list of people—family, friends, acquaintances—from whom I felt I might be able to borrow money. If I couldn't get one person to loan me $19,000 then maybe I could get nineteen people to loan me $1,000 each, or three to loan me $5,000 each and four to loan $1,000 each. The plan simply had to add up to $19,000, no matter how I got it.

6. The hardest part about Now Applying the Plan, the NAP principle, was that I had to admit to myself, to my wife, and others that I had made a poor decision based on my own greed. Once I had dealt with my ego and pride, all that was left was to begin talking to people and asking them for help,

signing notes, and then working hard to make the money to pay these good people back.

The fascinating thing is that some of the greatest lessons I have learned about business, life, and myself have been from this difficult situation. A helpful motto is: "No matter what is going on in your life, remember God does not play dirty tricks on you. He is in the business of building you and maturing you, and occasionally the process hurts."

SCRIPTURE REFERENCES TO DECISION MAKING

"Yes, if you want better insight and discernment, and are searching for them as you would for lost money or hidden treasure, then wisdom will be given you, and knowledge of God himself; you will soon learn the importance of reverence for the Lord and of trusting him" (Proverbs 2:3-5).

"In everything you do, put God first, and he will direct you and crown your efforts with success" (Proverbs 3:6).

"Have two goals: wisdom—that is, knowing and doing right—and common sense. Don't let them slip away, for they will fill you with living energy, and are a feather in your cap" (Proverbs 3:21, 22).

"Plans go wrong with too few counselors; many counselors bring success" (Proverbs 15:22).

"Do you know a hard-working man? He shall be successful and stand before kings!" (Proverbs 22:29).

FAMILIAR QUOTATIONS
ABOUT DECISION MAKING

"You won't be fired if you make a wrong decision," the president of an electronics firm tells his associates. "You'll only be fired if you make no decisions."

"You can judge a leader by the size of the problems he tackles—people nearly always pick a problem their own size.

and ignore or leave to others the bigger or smaller ones.''
—Anthony Jay

"The less one has to do, the less time one finds to do it in."
—Lord Chesterfield

"To think is to live."—Cicero

"It is easy to be critical. The real test is to come up with constructive alternatives.''—Anonymous

"Good judgment comes from experience. Experience comes from bad judgment.''—Anonymous

"Leadership is action—not position.''—Donald H. McGannon

"I must do something" will always solve more problems than "Something must be done."

"As one business leader recently put it: 'I want people around me who can solve problems, not recite facts.'''

PART FIVE
YOUR
PROSPERITY
PERSONALITY

THE BASIS OF ALL PROSPERITY

There is one concept that I would like everyone to carry in his mind, to examine from every angle as one does a beautiful diamond. That one matchless truth is that the basis of all prosperity is giving.

If you want to prosper *mentally* then don't just learn— determine also to teach. Teaching a subject is the way to really learn it. Teaching is the process of giving out of oneself and the subject material. As much benefit flows to the teacher as to the students.

Would you like to prosper *emotionally?* Find someone in need and reach out to help him. Paul said, "And I was a constant example to you in helping the poor; for I remembered the words of the Lord Jesus, 'It is more blessed to give than to receive'" (Acts 20:35).

More benefit flows to the giver than to the receiver. When we give of ourselves, certain emotions and feelings are let loose inside of us. Giving makes us vulnerable. We can be turned down when we try to give. We can be hurt, but being vulnerable isn't necessarily a bad thing. Without vulnerability love would be impossible. If we're afraid of being hurt we will never risk ourselves by reaching out.

An aged illustration in every preacher's file is about the Dead Sea, which is dead because it is always taking in and never giving out. If you want to be alive *spiritually* then you need to have some way you can give spiritually to others.

God makes it clear that there is blessing and happiness for those who give *materially* to help others. Paul spoke about financial giving: "Yes, God will give you much so that you can give away much, and when we take your gifts to those who need them they will break out into thanksgiving and praise to God for your help. So, two good things happen as a result of your gifts—those in need are helped, and they overflow with thanks to God. Those you help will be glad not only because of your generous gifts to themselves and to others, but they will praise God for this proof that your deeds are as good as your doctrine. And they will pray for you with deep fervor and feeling because of the wonderful grace of God shown through you'' (2 Corinthians 9:11-14).

I know people who have made lots of money but still understand very little about real prosperity.

MONEY TALK

It is still a fact that when people get their house in order financially one of the first things they ask is how they can do better for their family financially. I know this was true for me. One day after I had resigned my last pastorate I was going through files cleaning them out. There in a drawer were some photos of my children when they were little. They were dressed so shabbily that I was ashamed. It need not have been that way had I understood then what I know now about myself.

Once you get on a budget, you see things begin to happen that help you get straightened out financially. When you see you have three to six months cash available to you in liquid assets, you may want to think about some investments.

Again, I am not going to tell you where to invest. I'm not even going to tell you to do what I did. However, there are things I want you to be aware of before you start.

BEWARE OF TWO INCOMPATIBLE THINGS

There is a reason why some people make more money than others. There is a reason why some families argue and even end in divorce when one of the spouses gets ''crazy over money.''

Notice the illustration below:

$10,000
Mr. A. - - - - - - - - - (S.B.)

$10,000
Mr. B. - - - - - - - - - (S.B.)

In this illustration Mr. A. and Mr. B. each have $10,000 cash. I call this their *security base* (S.B.). Along comes an investment opportunity available to both of them. The person who controls the opportunity says that if one invests in $1,000 units, in one year—if the investment pans out—they will earn dollar for dollar. So this is how the two men respond to this *investment opportunity* (I.O.):

```
        $8,000                $2,000
Mr. A. - - - - - - - - (S.B.)  - - (I.O.)

        $2,000                $8,000
Mr. B. - - (S.B.)             - - - - - - - - (I.O.)
```

Mr. A. said, "I'll invest $2,000. So he buys two units for $2,000 investment opportunity (I.O.). Thus he reduces his security base (S.B.) to $8,000.

Mr. B. has a different makeup and attitude. "I came into the world with nothing—if I go out with nothing I haven't lost anything," he reasons, "so sell me eight of those units." In the illustration he invested $8,000.

For the sake of illustration, suppose the investment did pay dollar for dollar in one year. The result would be:

```
        $12,000
Mr. A. - - - - - - - - - - - - - (S.B.)

        $18,000
Mr. B. - - - - - - - - - - - - - - - - - - (S.B.)
```

Now let's say they are again confronted with the same kind of opportunity. Mr. A. says, "That wasn't too bad. I'll take another two units. If I lose them I will still have my original $10,000 left." Mr. B. says, "That was fun. Give me eighteen more units."

For the sake of illustration here is how it would look:

```
       $10,000 (S.B.)    $2,000 (I.O.)
Mr. A. - - - - - - - - - -    - -

       $0 (S.B.)         $18,000 (I.O.)
Mr. B. 0                 - - - - - - - - - - - - - - - - - -
```

Now Mr. A. has a $10,000 security base (S.B.) and again a $2,000 opportunity base (I.O.). Mr. B. has zero security and an $18,000 opportunity base (I.O.).

After a year the investment pays again dollar for dollar. Now take a look:

```
       $14,000 (S.B.)
Mr. A. - - - - - - - - - - - - - - -

       $36,000 (S.B.)
Mr. B. - - - - - - - - - - - - - - - - - - - - - - - - - - - - - - - - - -
```

Now Mr. A. has $14,000 but Mr. B. has $36,000, more than twice as much.

"But," you say, "Mr. B. could have lost everything if the investment had not worked as it did." Exactly! You are exactly right because the two things that cannot walk hand in hand are *opportunity* and *security*. When you reach out for opportunity you give up security. The amount of opportunity you reach for is the amount of security you give up. This explains why you and your spouse had better have some in-depth conversations before you start investing.

Some of the great battles in our marriage have been because one of us is opportunity-oriented and one is security-oriented. It will save you a lot of heartache and strained relationships, and may even save your marriage, if you will agree on what your investment personality is. You must decide how much security you are willing to give up to reach out for opportunity. Talk it over before you start. Then test the water and see how you feel.

The first thing you need to realize is that you shouldn't be afraid of the banker who must loan you money. That's right. Bankers must loan money to somebody so why shouldn't it be you? Money is all they have. If they are not lending money then they are not making any money. They make money by lending you money. They make it off the interest you pay on the money you have borrowed. All they have is money and, believe me, they want to lend it.

Next, realize that when you go to see your banker, someone is going to be in charge of the conversation. If possible, you should choose to be in control.

"How?" you ask. Remember that bankers are human. They have hearts, and they can be influenced, so start right. Clean yourself up—and your car. Bathe, shampoo, shine your shoes, and wear your best suit when you go to see the banker. "Eye appeal is half the deal," is a way my friend expresses it. When you walk up to the banker, all he knows about you is what he sees and you have only one chance to make a good first impression. In fact, I never go to the bank unless I am wearing a suit. I don't want my banker to think of me any other way than as a success. If I have to get some cash and I'm in old clothes I go to the drive-in window.

Never sit there in front of the banker and fill out the forms he may give you. Get several copies, take them home, use one copy for a worksheet, and type or carefully print the final statement you are going to submit to the banker.

When you go to see the banker, go with a plan. Don't just say you want money. Put down on paper the *subject,* what it is you want to do. Explain the *need,* how much money you need, and the *security,* or what you have to offer for collateral. State the *purpose,* what this loan will do for you, and the *terms.* Go ahead and ask for terms favorable to you. Finally state your *backup,* what you are planning to do in case everything fails, what you can do or sell to assure that the loan will eventually be paid back. Bankers love a backup.

Remember, uppermost in the mind of the banker is, "Can this person pay back this loan?" It has to be that way. It is the banker's business, so don't be afraid to ask.

WOULD YOU MAKE DECISIONS?

Before you ever go into business or try to secure your future with some type of investments, ask yourself the question, "Am I willing to make the hard decision?"

There are many reasons people make decisions, but let me list four very strong ones:

1. Ego. Some people seem to decide almost everything based on ego. This was the trap I was in for years. I kept telling myself and others that I would be doing something for the Lord but, as I look back, I see that all too often what I did was for myself. For example, I would find people with a problem and I would stay up any number of hours, give or lend them money, borrow money to give them, and even take them into my home. All this and more I did over and over in the name of my calling before God.

Now I can tell the truth. My self-image was so weak I didn't believe anyone liked me—not even my wife. So I would reach out to help someone, hoping that person would like me. If I continued to help him, I thought, maybe he would love me, and if I could get enough people to love me maybe I could love myself. Jesus made a strong statement about loving your neighbor as you love yourself. He wants us to love and accept ourselves.

2. Faith. Faith is a strong factor in people. There are those who give their lives for their faith. This is beautiful, and not to be taken lightly. But I often get tired of people who declare they are operating in the realm of faith when they are actually operating out of ego. Because I did so myself for so many years it may explain why I am oversensitive to this trait in others.

3. To feel good. Some people are highly motivated to feel good. I don't know another way to describe them. Much time is spent in eating right, exercising, weight-watching, anything to insure that they have the best possible chance to feel good. They will go to great lengths and pay any kind of money in their pursuit of feeling good. Lest you think I am exaggerating, go to any large city today and see how many

health spas and clubs are springing up everywhere.

4. Money. Money is a motivating factor for some people. Money itself is not evil. It is the love of money that is evil. Someone who is not sensitive to this will get his values twisted very quickly.

Ask yourself the following question; it is a good test of how you might make decisions:

Imagine you are in business and you have employed your wife's best girl friend, who is a member of your church and whose husband is a leader in the church. Suppose the woman is not performing at work and is costing you money? What are you going to do?

Your ego says to do the best you can with her, since you don't want to make your wife angry. Your so-called faith will allow you to stick with her. After all, you don't want to make a fuss in the church. There is no way any of this is going to make you feel good. On what do you base your decision?

You must do it based on the fact that she is causing you to lose money and if you keep on losing money you will soon be out of business. If you are not in business to make money you will soon be out of business. So the answer is that you must dismiss her.

The point of the whole story is simple. Investment involves risk and sometimes it is more than financial risks. Are you willing to make the hard decision?

17 / Moving Up

It has never fallen to my lot to be a corporate officer in a Fortune 500 company but I have learned some hard lessons on how to get along with management and how to move through the ranks.

FOLLOW SO YOU CAN LEAD

Before you can ever lead people you must learn to follow There is a time for you to keep still and do what leadership tells you to do.

You can probably think of people who are smart, gifted at their trade or profession, but who were never really considered for promotion. Some really gifted people stay in the lower echelons of a company for twenty or thirty years.

Allow me to suggest a reason why some people never move up. Suppose a man is a good machinist but his ego is out of control. A plan comes to his work bench and he studies it and is heard to say, "What a bunch of jerks these guys are who drew this plan. It will never work like this. If those college kids up there in the head office would ever come down here and ask us working stiffs how to do something, or better yet, if they let us run this place, things would get done."

Question: If you were in authority, would you promote this person? No, you wouldn't. He would cause you nothing but trouble. So a gifted person is passed over. To lead, you must learn to follow.

GET NEXT TO THOSE WHO ARE SUCCESSFUL

I believe enough in the American system of government and economics to think that people who choose to do so can better their lot in life. However not everyone will do so because not everyone will make such a choice. Those who do not want to pay the price to better their lives spiritually, mentally, physically, socially, or any other way never will help you.

Be willing to allow people to rise to the level of their own highest good. This principle has been one of the most difficult ones for me to accept. I'm constantly wanting people to do better for themselves than they seem to want to do.

As parents, our toughest assignment will be to allow our children to rise to the level of their own highest good. It might not be what we want, but we can't drag people where they do not want to go.

Recall the story of the rich young ruler who asked the Lord what he must do to inherit eternal life. When Jesus told him, he replied by his actions: "Then the man's face fell, and he went sadly away, for he was very rich" (Mark 10:22). Do you remember what Jesus did then for the young man? Not a thing. Not a thing! Jesus watched him walk out of his presence and did not call him back. Why? Because the gospel always makes us more responsible, not less responsible.

Learn the lesson well. You can't take people where they do not want to go, so allow people to rise to the level of their own highest good. Challenge them, lead them by example, but they must walk in the way. You can't drag them.

Moving through life you will find some people who have their lives in order and good things are happening for them and around them. Spend time with these people. One of my deepest regrets as pastor is that I took very little time for the best people because those with problems took so much time. Little did I realize that some of the problem people did not want answers.

You have only so much time and you can have only so many people in your life as friends, so pick the ones who are going to do something meaningful with their lives and spend your friendship time with them. But be sure you are doing something worthy also, or they may not want to take time for you.

LOOK RIGHT

Often at a seminar I will ask those who are gathered to look at me and then I ask, "Those of you who see me please raise your hand." Of course they all raise their hands. Half of them seem to suspect that it is a trick question but they can't figure out the trick.

Then I say, "No, you don't see me. The only part of me you see is my face and hands. All the rest is the package."

The way you package yourself makes a big difference as to how others perceive you. For years I was one of those people who would say, "I am me, the same person, whether I am in jeans or a suit. I'll dress the way I want to dress. If they are so good they don't like me the way I am, then they don't have to like me at all." How foolish I was!

A great day for me was when I bought John Molloy's book, *Dress for Success* (New York: Warner Books, 1978). It was an even greater day when I read it, believed it, and decided it was time to re-package myself and to do it right. Not only did others begin to look upon me more favorably but I began to look on myself with more favor. It is again a question of self-image.

The book tells about a test done with a green suit. A man was sent to borrow money wearing a green suit. He couldn't get anywhere in the green suit so he changed clothes and the loan officers changed their attitudes immediately and gave him the loan.

Now if I had read that story a few years ago I would probably have looked all over town to find a green suit and try to borrow money while wearing it, just to prove Molloy wrong. Not anymore. I have learned my lesson. Thank God, it is not too late for me to be a follower so I can earn the privilege of leading.

THE PRINCIPLE OF O.P.M.

If you have read anything about investments you have come across the principle of O.P.M. (Other People's Money). This principle is often discussed when people are being encouraged to use the principle of leverage to build a financial future for themselves.

For years I have worked at the job of building borrowing relationships with people. If you should ever feel you want to begin this type of relationship with people, then please understand you must never use O.P.M. for living expenses. You use other people's money only, only when you are able to earn money with the borrowed money and can be assured of paying the money back as agreed with generous interest. When you do, you have earned money both for you and the lender.

If you follow the principle of using O.P.M., then you must always keep some assets that you can liquidate in order to pay back the money. In my experience other people's money becomes more than a business agreement. Many times the basis for it is a long-time relationship too sacred to destroy with careless risks.

IS SUCCESS "CHRISTIAN"?

Matthew recorded Jesus as saying: "In that way you will be acting as true sons of your Father in heaven. For he gives his sunlight to both the evil and the good, and sends rain on the just and on the unjust too.'' That passage has always in-trigued me. It seems to be saying that God has set in motion principles that will always work, for the good and for the evil. We sometimes fail to realize that the secular man has taken some biblical principles and done better in applying them to his own advantage than we have applied them to ourselves and to the kingdom of God.

It is a fact that to lead you must follow. In washing the disciples' feet Jesus represented the submissive spirit of a great leader. Each one of the disciples whom Jesus called was evidently successful in his own business before Jesus called him. Jesus took good people and made them better. The Master did not surround himself with what we would call losers. Even Judas had ability to be chosen treasurer for the Lord's company of disciples. He simply made the wrong choice about Jesus.

Nothing in this chapter about moving up is contrary to the Word of God, but is rather a statement of biblical concepts that the unregenerate man has taken, secularized, and used to his own end. In that regard Jesus said correctly, ''And it is true that the citizens of this world are more clever [in dishonesty] than the godly are'' (Luke 16:8).

18 / Don't Look Back! Look Ahead!

My mother and father never did seem to get along well. I've heard mother tell how she married at an early age, became pregnant shortly after that, but never found much happiness in the relationship. Because they weren't getting along, she said, the two of them agreed that they would divorce as soon as their firstborn son, John, was out of high school. But other children came along until there were ten of us. Two died in infancy and there were several miscarriages. Each time there was another agreement—as soon as that child finished high school they would get a divorce.

I was the tenth child, and when I got out of high school, true to their word, they got a divorce. Married forty-two years and divorced! The sad part was that they had both so mellowed in old age that I'm sure they could have had some good years together if they had left the door closed on the past.

As I write this I am fast approaching forty-six years old. By today's standards that is not old, but I have enough miles on me to know that the way to live is by looking ahead, not back.

My prayer is, "Lord, keep me looking ahead, no matter what my age." I remember interviewing a lady in the lovely retirement center then called King's Garden—now called Crista. When I asked her how she liked her residence at King's Garden, she said, "Well, it's not like my own home but it's very nice." Then she went on, "This move was from my home to the King's Garden. My next move is going to be from the King's Garden to the King's Palace!"

You don't gain by looking back. Keep looking up and ahead. You are never too old to set goals and make plans.

MAKE THE REST OF YOUR LIFE
THE BEST OF YOUR LIFE

Retirement can be one of the best times of your life if you prepare for it. Make up your mind very early that you want to do something worthwhile with a portion of your retirement years.

While I was helping to pull together the loose ends of a mission organization, a man came to my office. He had been in management for a large company that made tin cans. His desire was to take his retirement, serve the Lord on a modest salary, and invest a portion of his life in the cause of Christ.

At that time the mission organization was promoting their first mobile medical clinic. I had an afternoon radio show at the time and used that show basically to raise the dollars for purchase and equipment for the mobile clinic.

This newly retired executive seemed perfect for the detail work of drawing together all the pieces of the clinic project. I asked him to call a man who was the most talented person with his hands that I know—one of those people who can do anything. He was also retired.

To make a long story short, these two retired men put that mobile clinic together and several other units after that. They have been to exotic places in the world delivering those mobile clinics, to places that others have only thought about and read about. But they have been there because their lives have continued to be of service.

As a pastor of a church that also ran a Christian school,

I can't say enough for the retired men who kept that place running.

"Bill, some kid just tore the blackboard off the wall," I would say.

"Don't worry, Pastor, I'll come down and fix it."

"Dale, we have two broken windows out back."

"All right, brother, I'll get to them."

I have often thought of Noah, to whom God spoke one day to give him instructions to build the ark. Noah went out to build and to serve God for the next 120 years. Then God spoke again. The Bible doesn't say whether or not God said anything during those 120 years, but it doesn't appear that he had to come around every few weeks to tell Noah to get back to work on the ark. Noah just did it because he was an obedient person. When we retire, we don't retire from God. He still wants us to be obedient.

RETIREMENT—A TIME OF FREEDOM
I've met too many retired people who look upon their retirement as freedom from work. May I challenge your thinking to look upon retirement as freedom to learn, to live, and to serve. Retirement allows us to put new priorities on our time.

Some missionaries would love to have a retired person come and help with the practical things so they can get on with the spiritual ministries. It is true that many boards don't allow even their older missionaries to stay on the field when they get to the place physically where they are a liability to the work rather than a help. But many retired people are still in good health—body, mind, and spirit. Mission boards are learning that we have the responsibility to preach, but that we have to earn the right to be heard. Some of that earning of the right to speak is done in very practical ways such as building, moving, digging, repairing, growing, feeding—things that can be done by retired people.

All your life you have prayed for missions and given to

missions. Now that you are about to retire, why not get busy and give to missions a few of those great years you have left?

In fact, you don't even need to go overseas. Your pastor and local church would be happy to save a slice of your time that they could invest in worthy service, provided you understand the true nature of service and ministry and are willing to stay within your capabilities and limitations. I know a man who was a very intelligent college professor and missionary. In his retirement he was enough of a servant and committed to the work of Christ to give several hours a day sorting mail, arranging letters in zip-code order, for a Christian organization.

Get beyond the idea that retirement is doing nothing. Start planning for some of the greatest times of your life. I like the ninety-six-year-old lady in Ohio who was hurrying across the street because she didn't want to be late for an appointment.

"Where are you going?" I shouted as she strode by.

Her answer stunned me. "I'm due at the nursing home to help read to some old people."

YOU CAN DO IT

There is not anything in this book that you can't do. You can change your self-image; you can set goals; you can budget; you can make the tough decision; and you can live with a prosperous outlook on life.

One thing will keep you from it. It is a principle I call "creative avoidance." You create things to avoid doing what you know you should be doing. For instance, did you know it is possible to sharpen pencils for twenty minutes every day before you start to write material for a book like this? Believe me, I know. I've done it. The embarrassing thing is that after I've spent twenty minutes sharpening pencils, I do my writing on a typewriter.

Those things you always wanted to do—believe me, you

can do them. Just keep at it. Your course will not always be up. Progress is not continual for any of us. We all have our good times and our bad times, but don't ever give up on yourself. I know you can do it. I'd like to meet you someday in one of my seminars. I want you to come up and say, "Hi, Lanson. Look at me. I'm living a prosperous and happy life."

SCRIPTURE REFERENCES
TO YOUR PROSPERITY PERSONALITY

"You will be given the sense to stay away from evil men who want you to be their partners in crime—men who turn from God's ways to walk down dark and evil paths, and exult in doing wrong, for they thoroughly enjoy their sins" (Proverbs 2:11-13).

"Follow the steps of the godly instead, and stay on the right path, for only good men enjoy life to the full; evil men lose the good things they might have had, and they themselves shall be destroyed" (Proverbs 2:20-22).

"For if you give, you will get! Your gift will return to you in full and overflowing measure, pressed down, shaken together to make room for more, and running over. Whatever measure you use to give—large or small—will be used to measure what is given back to you" (Luke 6:38).

"For God, who gives seed to the farmer to plant, and later on, good crops to harvest and eat, will give you more and more seed to plant and will make it grow so that you can give away more and more fruit from your harvest. Yes, God will give you much so that you can give away much, and when we take your gifts to those who need them they will break out into thanksgiving and praise to God for your help" (2 Corinthians 9:10, 11).

FAMILIAR QUOTATIONS ABOUT
YOUR PROSPERITY PERSONALITY

"The Spartans do not enquire how many the enemy are, but where they are."—Agis II, 427 B.C.

"The work of the world does not wait to be done by perfect people."—Anonymous

"The older I get the more wisdom I find in the ancient rule of taking first things first—a process which often reduces the most complex human problems to manageable proportion."—Dwight D. Eisenhower

"The higher you go the more dependent you become on others."—Anonymous

"Don't be misled into believing that somehow the world owes you a living. The boy who believes that his parents, or the government, or anyone else owes him his livelihood and that he can collect it without labor will wake up one day and find himself working for another boy who did not have that belief and, therefore, earned the right to have others work for him."—David Sarnoff

"Act with a determination not to be turned aside by thoughts of the past and fears of the future."—Robert E. Lee

A youth was questioning a lonely old man. "What is life's heaviest burden?" he asked. The old fellow answered sadly, "To have nothing to carry."—Anonymous

"Remember that today is your opportunity. Tomorrow is some other fellow's."—William Feather

"Remember, it takes more than money to build a future."—Anonymous